D0485289

Viennese Desserts
Made Easy

Viennese Desserts
Made Easy

Georgina Gronner

Contemporary Books, Inc.
Chicago

Library of Congress Cataloging in Publication Data

Gronner, Georgina.
   Viennese desserts made easy.

   Includes index.
   1. Desserts.   2. Cookery, Austrian.   I. Title.
TX773.G699   1983   641.8′6′0943613   82-22109
ISBN 0-8092-5621-5 (pbk.)

Published by Contemporary Books, Inc.
180 North Michigan Avenue, Chicago, Illinois 60601
Manufactured in the United States of America
Library of Congress Catalog Card Number: 82-22109
International Standard Book Number: 0-8092-5621-5

Published simultaneously in Canada by
Beaverbooks, Ltd.
150 Lesmill Road
Don Mills, Ontario M3B 2T5
Canada

To the memory of my husband, Robert Gronner

Contents

Introduction

The Deliciously Simple Art of Baking

There is no mystery to baking delicious pastries. So many times friends say to me, "I love to cook but I'm afraid to bake. I know it would take too much time and my pastry wouldn't be as good as store-bought." Happily, some of these people have taken my pastry course and learned how wrong they were. Many of my former students now wouldn't dream of buying pastries.

Why the dramatic switch? Because I shared with them a few simple secrets about baking. First, even if you don't keep strict rules in baking, what you put in will come out. As long as you use top quality ingredients, adding a bit more flour or sugar or one less egg to a recipe won't matter. It will still come out satisfactorily. Baking shouldn't be compulsive—you can be flexible with recipes. I encourage novices to add flavorings to *their* taste.

Second, if you plan wisely, baking needn't be time-consuming. Many of my recipes can be made in stages, and most of the pastries (except yeast breads) and creams improve in flavor with a few days' aging. I will tell you a little bit later how to bake an elegant dessert buffet for fifty in only one day! Planning is the key.

Third, no matter what you buy in a pastry shop, it will never match the flavor of homemade pastry. I say this with such confidence because it stands to reason that no commercial bakery can afford to use the quality ingredients you will use in your home-baked pastries.

These recipes are my variations of Viennese favorites passed down from my mother and grandmother. They range from party creations like Chocolate Chestnut Marzipan Delight to flavorful family desserts such as Open-Faced Apple Tart. Of course, I've included all the classics, such as Linzer Torte, Ischler Cookies, and Sacher Torte—but with my own special touches. I challenge anyone to find a moister Sacher Torte than my grandmother's recipe will provide.

When I was growing up, we had a big household with a cook in the kitchen, a maid in the living room and bedrooms, and a nurse in the children's rooms. It was my mother's job to see that each one stayed in her own territory. This especially applied to the children who were supposed to be in school, playing in the park, or doing their homework. In other words, the kitchen was off limits to me unless I wanted a glass of water or a chance to gossip with the cook when my parents weren't at home. So, when I married, I had absolutely no knowledge of baking, but I did have a love of sweets and lots of nerve.

With some experimentation I discovered that if you follow a few basic rules—creaming butter and sugar first, then adding egg yolks and flour, then folding in stiffly beaten egg whites—it's hard to go wrong. I've had gratifying results with baking ever since. I am amused when people say how "professional" my pastries are. I know that any cook can turn out the same quality, and it's my hope that with the help of this book you will.

As my friend Mary Still says, "Eating pastry is so *gemütlich* (a happy combination of cheer and comfort) because it brings people together."

1

Recommended Ingredients

As I said earlier, "What you put in is what comes out." If you use only the finest quality ingredients you'll taste the difference. Consult the following list before shopping.

Butter. Buy unsalted butter, which is sometimes labeled "sweet." Salt is a preservative that can mask the flavor of slightly rancid butter. Butter can be frozen for up to six months, so stock up if you see some on sale. Defrost frozen butter in the refrigerator before using. Most of the recipes call for butter at room temperature, which means it should be soft enough to beat easily.

Cake and Cookie Crumbs. Any leftover or stale cake or cookie crumbs should be processed in a food processor fitted with a steel blade or in a blender to make fine crumbs. The crumbs can be frozen in a well-sealed container. Several of my cake recipes use crumbs instead of flour for added flavor.

Chocolate. I recommend semisweet chocolate morsels because it's the easiest type of cooking chocolate to work with. Since it's already shaped into small pieces and has a high cocoa butter content, it melts quickly. Its sugar content gives it a lovely sheen when it sets. (See Chapter 3, "Tips and Techniques," for suggestions on melting chocolate.)

> *Chocolate Sprinkles.* Tiny chocolate candies used for cake and cookie decorations. These can be purchased in most supermarkets.
>
> *Cocoa.* I prefer "Dutch process" cocoa which has a darker color and mellower flavor than regular cocoa.

Citrus Juices and Peel. I use frozen orange juice concentrate and fresh-squeezed lemon juice. When lemon or orange peel is called for, always use fresh—it has a much better flavor than dried peel. (To grate citrus peel see Chapter 2, "Equipment," under Citrus Zester.)

Eggs. Grade A large. Leftover egg whites can be stored in a container in the refrigerator for several weeks or frozen for up to six months. For use in recipes, 6 egg whites weigh approximately 6 ounces and measure ¾ of a cup.

Flour. I use all-purpose presifted flour for all my pastries. Some brands come in a convenient shaker container which is handy for dusting pans and work surfaces with flour.

Jams. Raspberry and apricot jam are used in many of the recipes. It's nice to keep a supply in the pantry for impromptu baking.

Liquors and Liqueurs. Always use real liquors and liqueurs. The artificial extracts taste terrible. Following are the liquors I use in baking: rum, cognac, bourbon, coffee liqueur, chocolate liqueur, and orange liqueur. Of course, you don't need all of these in your cabinet. I recommend substitutions in the recipes.

In recipes calling for wine, use a dry or semisweet table wine, not cooking wine.

Nuts. Buy nuts in bulk, if possible, from a store with a rapid turnover. The cost will be cheaper and the nuts will be fresher. Nuts can be stored, tightly covered, in the freezer for up to six months. Many of my recipes call for ground nuts (see Chapter 2, "Equipment," and Chapter 3, "Tips and Techniques").

> *Almonds.* Unless otherwise specified in recipe, use whole unblanched almonds.
>
>> BLANCHED ALMONDS. Almonds with the dark outer skin removed (see instructions in Chapter 3, "Tips and Techniques").
>>
>> SLIVERED ALMONDS. Blanched almonds cut into very thin slices which are used for decoration. These should be purchased already slivered.
>>
>> ALMOND PASTE OR MARZIPAN. A mixture of ground almonds, egg white, and sugar. It can be bought in bulk and will keep in the refrigerator for weeks.
>
> *Chestnuts.* Canned chestnut puree (*crème de marrons vanillée*) is available in import food shops.
>
> *Hazelnuts.* Hazelnuts must be peeled before using in recipes. I prefer to buy hazelnuts with the skin on and peel them myself (see instructions in Chapter 3, "Tips and Techniques). For some reason, the peeled hazelnuts I've bought lack flavor.
>
> *Walnuts.* Buy either in the shell or already shelled. Walnuts don't need to be peeled before using.

Bulk nuts, almond paste, and chestnut puree can be ordered by mail from:

> Meyer Delicatessen Import
> 3306 N. Lincoln Ave.
> Chicago, IL 60657

Raisins. Two types are used: golden and dark. After raisins are opened, store in a well-sealed container in a cool spot.

Sugar. "Sugar" listed in a recipe means granulated. Confectioners' sugar (also called powdered sugar) will be specified.

Vanilla Extract and Vanilla Bean. Use real extract for the best flavor. Fresh vanilla beans, which are long, skinny, dark brown pods, can be purchased in import food shops.

Whipping Cream. Sometimes labeled "heavy" cream. Avoid ultra-pasteurized whipping cream because it takes longer to whip and has a slightly cooked flavor.

2

Equipment

These are the tools and baking pans you will need for my pastry recipes.

Electric Mixer. Indispensable as a time and effort saver.

Food Processor. Very good for chopping and grinding nuts and mixing batters. All of the cake recipes in the book can be mixed in the processor, if desired, according to one basic procedure: If nuts are called for in the recipe, always grind them first when the bowl is clean and dry. Then add butter, sugar, and melted chocolate. While the machine is running, add egg yolks through the feed tube and process 1 to 2 minutes more. Add flour and any flavorings last. For greatest volume, the egg whites should be beaten with an electric mixer, then folded into the batter.

Blender. Can be used for chopping and grinding nuts.

Nut Grinder. Good for grinding nuts and chocolate.

Citrus Zester (see illustration). A handy little tool for removing the peel of lemons and oranges in thin strips. It removes just the colored outer skin and not the bitter white under-skin. The strips can then be chopped fine for use in recipes. If you don't have a citrus zester, the peel can be grated on the fine side of a 4-sided vegetable grater/slicer. Use a pastry brush to remove peel that sticks to the grater.

The Decorating Comb is a jagged-edged metal triangle that is used for making designs on top of cakes and petits fours. *The Fluted Pastry Wheel* is a jagged-edged metal wheel set into a wooden handle. It is used to cut pastry strips for lattice-topped tarts. *The Citrus Zester* is a metal plate with small, sharp holes in the end that is set into a plastic handle. The zester removes the peel of lemons and oranges in long, thin strips.

4-Sided Vegetable Grater/Slicer. Good for slicing apples for tarts and for grating citrus peel (see above).

Pastry Brush. Useful for covering cakes with jams and spreading icings on petits fours and cookies. Buy a brush with natural bristles.

Pastry Bag and a Variety of Decorating Tips. Use for decorating cakes and for forming and filling cream puffs. I like the pastry bag that is made of cloth on the outside (for a firm grip) and plastic inside (for easy cleaning). After using, wash the bag in warm soapy water, rinse well, and allow to air dry.

Fluted Pastry Wheel (see illustration). Makes a pretty edge on pastry strips for lattice-top tarts.

Rolling Pin. Buy the biggest size you can easily handle, preferably with ball bearings in the handle. This kind of pin makes rolling pastry easier because the ball bearings do most of the work.

Rubber Spatulas and Metal Spatulas. Rubber spatulas are good for scraping bowls and for folding beaten egg whites into cake batter. Metal spatulas (about 8 to 10 inches long) are useful for spreading buttercreams and smoothing icings on cakes.

Decorating Comb (see illustration). Used for making designs on top of cakes and petits fours. The combs are available in kitchen supply stores and stores that sell cake-decorating items.

Small Fine Sieve or Dredger. Handy for sprinkling confectioners' sugar over cakes and pastries.

Aluminum Foil. Used for lining some cake pans and for wrapping frozen or refrigerated pastries.

Thin Metal Skewer. Inserted into the center of a cake to test for doneness. If the skewer comes out dry, that means the cake is baked.

Oven Thermometer. Not absolutely necessary but it can provide some baking insurance. Often baking flops occur because the actual oven temperature varies from the setting on the temperature gauge. To use the thermometer, place it in the oven and preheat oven for 15 minutes. Check temperature on thermometer. If actual temperature varies from the temperature gauge setting, adjust the gauge up or down accordingly.

Suggested Baking Pans. Buy good, heavy quality aluminum or steel pans.

> 9-inch springform pan
> 10-inch springform pan
> 10-inch bundt pan
> 12" × 4" × 2½" loaf pan
> 10" × 4½" × 1¾" fluted cake pan (Bischofsbrot pan)
> 15" × 10" × 1½" jelly-roll pan
> 17" × 12" × 2" jelly-roll pan
> several cookie sheets
> 6-cup steamed pudding mold with hinged top (other 6-cup mold can be substituted, see recipe, page 94)
> 10" × 6" baking dish
> 10-inch soufflé dish
> 9" or 10" frying pan
> 5-cup ring mold

Wire Cooling Rack. Good for cooling cakes, pies, and cookies because it allows air to circulate around the baked goods. If you don't have a wire rack, sprinkle a surface lightly with confectioners' sugar and place the cake or cookies on the sugar.

3

Tips and Techniques

These suggestions are designed to save you time and effort and to make the art of baking more enjoyable.

Beating Egg Whites. Always beat egg whites in a clean bowl with an electric mixer, just until stiff peaks form. As soon as egg whites are beaten they should be folded into the already mixed cake batter. All of my recipes are written following this procedure; however, when I bake, I beat the egg whites first and set them aside. Then, working very quickly with premeasured ingredients, I mix the basic batter using the same beaters (saves washing them). I then fold the egg whites into the batter. Because I work so quickly, the egg whites don't have time to lose any air. If you're the type of cook who can work quickly, you might want to try this time-saving method. If you work slowly, you can put the beaten egg whites in the refrigerator while you mix the batter.

Folding Egg Whites. Beaten egg whites must be folded into batter quickly so that air trapped in them is not lost. To fold the egg whites, first place them on top of the batter. Using a large rubber spatula, start at the center of the bowl and, working toward the outer edge of the bowl, lift the batter up and over the whites. At the same time, rotate the bowl with your other hand. Continue this simultaneous motion until all the batter is incorporated into the beaten egg whites. Pour the mixture gently into the prepared baking pan and bake right away.

Whipping Cream. Make sure cream is ice cold. On hot summer days, it's a good idea to chill the bowl and beaters. Whip until soft peaks form, then gradually add the specified amount of sugar, while continuing to whip. Whip until the cream holds stiff peaks (do not overwhip or cream will turn to butter). Cream can be whipped several hours in advance of serving, covered and refrigerated.

Peeling Nuts.

Almonds. Blanching is the easiest way to remove almond skins. Bring a pan of water to the boil and put in shelled almonds. Remove from heat and let almonds sit for 3 to 4 minutes. Strain almonds in a colander, then remove skins with your fingertips. Spread the skinned almonds on a towel to dry for a few minutes before storing or using.

Hazelnuts. To skin hazelnuts, spread shelled nuts in a single layer on a baking sheet. Toast the nuts in a preheated 350° F. oven or a toaster oven until the skins start to blister (about 8 to 10 minutes). Remove from oven and spread nuts on a towel. Rub nuts between folds of towel to remove skins. Any clinging pieces of skin can be removed with your fingernails or a small, sharp knife, but don't be fanatical. If a few small pieces of skin remain, that's OK.

Chopping and Grinding Nuts. Nuts can be chopped with a large chef's knife, a blender, or food processor. To chop nuts in the processor, put the steel blade and nuts in the workbowl. Process with on/off technique until nuts are desired consistency.

Nuts can be ground with a nut grinder, a blender, or food processor. To grind nuts in the processor, continue with an on/off technique until nuts are a fine powder. Do not overprocess or nuts will turn to nut butter.

Melting Chocolate. Because I use semisweet chocolate I never bother with melting it in a double boiler. I melt chocolate by putting it in a heavy pan or heat-proof bowl and placing it in the oven just as I turn it on to preheat it. In a few minutes I take it out and it's beautifully melted. You can also melt chocolate on the stovetop in a heavy pan over very low heat. Remove it from the heat just as soon as it melts—you don't want to cook it.

Organization. Organization is important to successful baking. Have all ingredients out and measured before you begin mixing and you will find that the actual mixing goes very quickly.

4

Cakes and Tortes

The cakes and tortes of my native city, Vienna, are justly renowned all over the world. Most Viennese cakes are leavened by nothing more than air whipped into the egg whites and egg yolks, which results in light and tender cakes.

When sliced into thin layers, then filled and covered with a delectable assortment of buttercreams, jams, chestnut puree, marzipan, chocolate, and whipped cream, they become edible works of art. The tortes are especially flavorful and moist because cake crumbs or ground nuts are substituted for flour in the batter.

In some of my recipes, I leave the choice of buttercream and icing flavor up to the cook—so you can create masterpieces to your own taste. And with my decorating hints, your cake will look as wonderful as it tastes.

These cakes and tortes are festive desserts that provide the crowning touch to any special occasion, but you don't need a celebration to merit one of them. Bake one of these beauties and the cake itself becomes the occasion!

Lemon Cake Roll Petits Fours
(Petits Fours aus Zitronenroulade)   MAKES 28 SERVINGS

The first time that you roll the cake into two small rolls you may be overanxious and have problems, but relax, it's really quite easy.

Lemon Cake Roll with Buttercream Filling (following
    recipe)
1 recipe desired icing (see Chapter 9)

1.   Prepare cake as in basic recipe through Step 2.
2.   Start on a long side of the cake, roll the foil and cake into a spiral to the center of the cake. Repeat with other half (see illustration). Let cake cool. Cut cake in half to form two long rolls. Unroll each one and remove foil.
3.   Prepare desired buttercream. Divide the buttercream between the two cakes and frost. Roll each cake jelly-roll fashion.
4.   Prepare desired icing. Pour icing over each cake roll. Let icing set, then cut each roll into 14 slices. Place slices into small paper cups before serving.

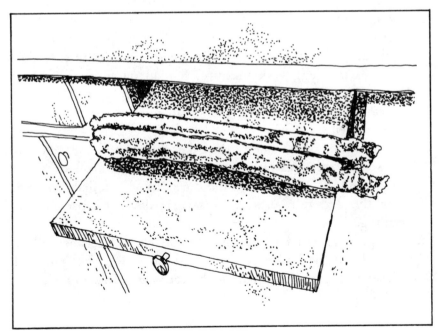

Starting with a long side of the cake, roll foil and cake tightly to the center.

Repeat with other half of cake. Let cake cool.

Lemon Cake Roll with Buttercream Filling
(*Zitronenroulade*)   MAKES 14 SERVINGS

These cake rolls look so impressive and taste so delicious that your guests will never guess they take less than one hour—start to finish—to make.

The cake rolls can be made into one large roll as a sit-down dessert or into two smaller rolls* for dessert buffet petits fours (see Chapter 10, "Plan a 'Baking Day' for a Special Party").

6 eggs, separated
½ cup sugar
⅓ cup flour
Peel of ½ lemon, grated
1 recipe desired buttercream (see Chapter 9)

1. Preheat oven to 350°F. Line a 15″ × 10½″ × 1½″ baking pan with aluminum foil. Butter and flour foil. Set aside.

2. Beat egg yolks, sugar, flour, and lemon peel until fluffy (about 3 minutes). Set aside. Beat egg whites until stiff. Fold whites into egg yolk mixture. Spread on prepared baking pan. Bake in preheated 350°F. oven until cake starts to come away from sides of pan (about 10 minutes). Remove cake from oven.

3. Starting on a long side of the cake, roll the foil and cake into a spiral (see illustration). Let cake cool. Unroll cake and remove foil. At this point the cake can be rerolled, wrapped tightly, and refrigerated for several days or frozen before filling.

4. Prepare desired buttercream. Unroll cake. Use about three fourths of the buttercream to frost cake. Roll cake jelly-roll fashion. Frost with remaining buttercream. To serve, cut into 14 slices.

---

*Only the Chocolate Cake Roll cannot be made into two smaller rolls because it will crack.

Orange Cake Roll with Orange Filling
(Orangenroulade)   MAKES 14 SERVINGS

 6 eggs, separated
 1 cup sugar
 1 cup flour
 Peel of 1 orange, grated
 2 tablespoons frozen orange juice concentrate, thawed
 Orange Filling (recipe follows)

1.   Preheat oven to 350°F. Line a 15″ × 10½″ × 1½″ baking pan with aluminum foil. Butter and flour foil. Set aside.

2.   Beat egg yolks, sugar, flour, orange peel, and orange juice until fluffy (about 3 minutes). Set aside. Beat egg whites until stiff. Fold into reserved batter. Spread on prepared baking pan. Bake in preheated 350°F. oven until cake starts to come away from sides of pan (about 10 minutes). Remove cake from oven.

3.   Follow procedures in Steps 3 and 4 of Lemon Cake Roll with Buttercream Filling (see Index), substituting Orange Filling for the buttercream.

Orange Filling

 4 egg yolks
 2 tablespoons frozen orange juice concentrate,
     thawed
 ½ cup butter, at room temperature
 1 tablespoon rum

1.   Over low heat (preferably in a nonstick pan), cook egg yolks with orange juice, stirring constantly with a wooden spoon, until mixture thickens. Remove from heat and set aside to cool.

2.   In the same bowl the cake was mixed in (saves washing a bowl), beat butter until fluffy. Add egg yolk and orange juice mixture and beat until fluffy. Mix in rum. Chill for 30 minutes or longer.

Orange Cake Roll Petits Fours
(Petits Fours aus Orangenroulade)   MAKES 28 SERVINGS

Orange Cake Roll with Orange Filling (preceding
    recipe)
Orange Icing (recipe follows)

1.   Make Orange Cake Roll through Step 2 of basic recipe.
2.   Follow procedure in Steps 3 and 4 of Lemon Cake Roll Petits
     Fours (see Index), substituting Orange Filling and Orange
     Icing for desired buttercream and icing.

Orange Icing

2 cups confectioners' sugar
4 tablespoons frozen orange juice concentrate,
    thawed
1 tablespoon butter, at room temperature

In a heavy saucepan boil sugar and orange juice until
mixture coats the back of a spoon. Let cool to lukewarm.
Beat in butter.

Chocolate Cake Roll with Buttercream Filling
(Schokoladenroulade)   MAKES 14 SERVINGS

½ cup semisweet chocolate morsels
2 tablespoons butter
6 eggs, separated
¼ cup sugar
½ cup blanched almonds, ground
3 tablespoons flour
1 recipe desired buttercream (see Chapter 9)

1. Preheat oven to 350°F. Line a 15″ × 10½″ × 1½″ baking pan with aluminum foil. Butter and flour foil. Set aside.
2. Melt chocolate and butter. Beat egg yolks, sugar, almonds, flour, chocolate, and butter until fluffy (about 3 minutes). Set aside. Beat egg whites until stiff. Fold whites into reserved batter. Spread on prepared baking pan. Bake in preheated 350°F. oven until cake starts to come away from sides of pan (about 10 minutes). Remove cake from oven.
3. Follow procedure in Steps 3 and 4 of Lemon Cake Roll with Buttercream Filling (see Index).

   Note: Do not divide this recipe into two small rolls. The chocolate crumbles easily when rolled that tightly.

Walnut Cake Roll with Buttercream Filling
(Nussroulade) MAKES 14 SERVINGS*

    5 eggs, separated
    ½ cup sugar
    ½ cup walnuts, ground
    ⅓ cup flour
    1 recipe desired buttercream (see Chapter 9)

1. Preheat oven to 350°F. Line a 15″ × 10½″ × 1½″ baking pan with aluminum foil. Butter and flour foil. Set aside.
2. Beat egg yolks, sugar, walnuts, and flour until fluffy (about 3 minutes). Set aside. Beat egg whites until stiff. Fold whites into reserved batter. Spread on prepared baking pan. Bake in preheated 350°F. oven until cake starts to come away from sides of pan (about 10 minutes). Remove cake from oven.
3. Follow procedure in Steps 3 and 4 of Lemon Cake Roll with Buttercream Filling (see Index).

-----

*To make Walnut Cake Roll Petits Fours (*Petits Fours aus Nussroulade*), follow instructions for Lemon Cake Roll Petits Fours (see Index), substituting Walnut Cake for Lemon Cake.

Almond Poppyseed Cake
(Mohntorte mit Mandeln)   MAKES 16 SERVINGS

This recipe can be varied by substituting coffee or chocolate icing for the orange. Or if you're really in a hurry, this moist cake is just fine served with a sprinkling of confectioners' sugar on top.

2 cups almonds, ground
¾ cup butter or margarine, at room temperature
½ cup sugar
6 eggs, separated
Peel of 1 lemon, grated
Peel of 1 orange, grated
Juice of 1 lemon
1 12½-ounce can poppyseed filling
2 teaspoons cinnamon
¼ cup apricot jam
1 recipe Orange Icing (see Index)

Garnish
   Chocolate sprinkles
   Slivered almonds

1. Preheat oven to 350°F. Butter and flour a 10-inch springform pan. Set aside.
2. If almonds are ground in food processor, leave them in workbowl and add butter, sugar, egg yolks, citrus peels, lemon juice, poppyseed, and cinnamon. Process to combine well (about 3 to 4 minutes), scraping down sides of bowl as necessary. If nuts are ground in a nut grinder, grind and set aside. Cream the butter and sugar until light and fluffy. Add egg yolks, almonds, citrus peels, lemon juice, poppyseed, cinnamon, and ground nuts. Mix well to combine. Set aside.
3. Beat egg whites until stiff. Fold into reserved batter and pour

into prepared baking pan. Bake in preheated 350°F. oven until thin skewer inserted in center comes out clean (about 1½ hours). Remove to wire rack to cool.

4. When cake is cool, slice into two layers. Cover bottom layer with apricot jam. Top with remaining layer. Cover top and sides with orange icing. Place a 4-inch-wide jar lid or other round form over center of cake. Cover cake top with chocolate sprinkles. Remove lid and garnish center circle with slivered almonds. To serve, cut into 16 wedges.

Sacher Torte à la Mutti   MAKES 16 SERVINGS

Madame Sacher originated this famous cake at the Hotel Sacher in Vienna. This version, based on my mother's recipe, is the best I've ever tasted.

1¼ cups semisweet chocolate morsels
1 cup butter or margarine
8 eggs, separated
1 cup sugar
1½ cups almonds, ground
2 tablespoons cake crumbs or flour
¼ cup apricot jam
1 recipe Chocolate Icing (see Index)

Garnish
Slivered almonds

Optional garnish
1 cup whipping cream whipped with 2 tablespoons
confectioners' sugar

1. Preheat oven to 350°F. Butter and flour a 10-inch springform pan. Set aside.
2. In a small, heavy saucepan, melt chocolate and butter over low heat. Set aside.
3. Beat egg yolks and sugar until light and fluffy (about 3 minutes). Mix in chocolate, butter, almonds, and cake crumbs. Set aside. Beat egg whites until stiff. Fold whites into batter, then pour into prepared pan. Bake in preheated 350°F. oven until skewer inserted comes out clean (about 60 minutes). Remove to wire rack to cool.
4. When cake is cool, brush top with apricot jam and cover with Chocolate Icing. Decorate top with slivered almonds. To serve, cut into 16 wedges. If desired, serve with sweetened whipped cream.

Variation: *Sacher Torte*

  Sacher Torte (preceding recipe)
  ½ recipe desired buttercream (see Chapter 9)
  1 recipe Chocolate Icing (see Index)

1. Prepare cake through Step 3 of basic recipe.
2. When cake is cool, slice into two layers and fill bottom layer with buttercream. Top with remaining layer and cover top and sides with Chocolate Icing.

Sourcream Citrus Cake
(Rahmkuchen zum Kaffee)

MAKES 16 SERVINGS

1 cup butter or margarine, at room temperature
1 cup sugar
4 eggs, separated
1 cup sour cream
1½ cups flour
1 teaspoon baking soda
1 teaspoon baking powder
Peel of 2 lemons, grated
Peel of 1 orange, grated
Orange Glaze (recipe follows)

1. Preheat oven to 350°F. Butter and flour a 10-inch springform pan. Set aside.
2. Cream butter and sugar until fluffy. Beat in egg yolks one at a time. Mix in sour cream. Combine flour, baking soda, and baking powder; mix into batter. Add citrus peels and mix. Set aside. Beat egg whites until stiff, then fold into batter. Pour into prepared pan and bake in preheated 350°F. oven until skewer inserted in center comes out clean (about 60 minutes). Remove to wire rack to cool.
3. Prepare Orange Glaze. Remove cake from pan and cover with glaze. To serve, cut into 16 wedges.

Orange Glaze

2 tablespoons butter, at room temperature
2 egg yolks
2 tablespoons frozen orange juice concentrate, thawed
Peel of 1 orange, grated
2 cups confectioners' sugar

Beat all ingredients together until smooth. Scrape sides of bowl several times while beating.

Cream Cheese Almond Torte
(*Topfenkuchen*)   MAKES 16 SERVINGS

This "Austrian style" cheesecake is moist and flavorful, yet light enough to enjoy after a meal.

½ cup butter or margarine, at room temperature
1 8-ounce package cream cheese, at room temperature
1 cup sugar
5 eggs, separated
1½ cups blanched almonds, ground
Peel of 1 lemon, grated
Peel of 1 orange, grated
3 tablespoons "Dutch process" cocoa
2 tablespoons flour
2 tablespoons rum

Garnish
Confectioners' sugar

1. Preheat oven to 350° F. Butter and flour a 10-inch springform pan. Set aside.
2. Cream butter and cream cheese until smooth. Add sugar and beat until smooth. Add egg yolks one at a time and beat until smooth. Mix in almonds, citrus peels, cocoa, flour, and rum. Mix to combine. Pour batter into prepared pan and bake in preheated 350° F. oven. Bake until skewer inserted in center comes out clean (about 45 minutes). Remove to wire rack to cool. When cool, remove from pan and dust top with confectioners' sugar. To serve, cut into 16 wedges.

Marzipan Torte
(Marzipantorte)
MAKES 16 SERVINGS

If you're pressed for time, don't beat the egg whites separately. Add the whole eggs where the egg yolks are added in Step 2 of the following recipe, then continue with the recipe. You'll sacrifice a bit of lightness but the flavor will still be wonderful.

½ cup sugar
½ cup butter or margarine, at room temperature
4 eggs, separated
1 cup almond paste
1 tablespoon kirsch
¼ cup flour
½ teaspoon baking powder
Peel of ½ lemon, grated

Garnish
    Confectioners' sugar

Optional garnish
    Raspberry Sauce (recipe follows)

1.   Preheat oven to 350° F. Butter and flour a 10-inch springform pan. Set aside.

2.   Cream butter and sugar until fluffy. Add egg yolks and beat until fluffy. Crumble almond paste into sugar and egg mixture, then beat at low speed until well combined. Add remaining ingredients except egg whites, confectioners' sugar, and Raspberry Sauce. Mix to combine. Set aside. Beat egg whites until stiff. Fold into reserved batter. Pour into prepared pan and bake in preheated 350° F. oven until skewer comes out clean (about 50 minutes). Remove to wire rack to cool.

3. When cake is cool, remove from pan and dust with confectioners' sugar. Cut into 16 wedges. Serve with Raspberry Sauce if desired.

Raspberry Sauce

    1 10-ounce package frozen raspberries, thawed
    1 cup whipping cream
    2 tablespoons confectioners' sugar

1. Process berries in food processor fitted with steel blade or in blender until pureed. Strain through fine sieve to remove seeds. Discard seeds; set puree aside.
2. Whip cream until soft peaks form. Continue whipping while gradually adding confectioners' sugar until stiff peaks form. Fold whipped cream into puree. Sauce can be refrigerated for several hours or served right away.

Variation   MAKES 16 SERVINGS

    Marzipan Torte (preceding recipe)
    2 tablespoons raspberry jam
    1 recipe Chocolate Icing (see Index)

1. Prepare torte through Step 2 in basic recipe.
2. When torte is cool, remove from pan and brush top and sides with raspberry jam. Cover top and sides of torte with Chocolate Icing. To serve, cut into 16 wedges.

Marzipan Orange Cake
(Marzipan Orangentorte)

This cake makes a good choice for a dinner party because it can be baked a day in advance. In fact, the flavor improves if made the day before. A couple of hours before serving, roll the marzipan layer and whip the cream for the frosting.

6 eggs, separated
¾ cup sugar
1⅓ cups flour
Marzipan Filling (recipe follows)
Whipped Cream Frosting (recipe follows)
⅓ cup raspberry jam
2 tablespoons orange liqueur or curaçao

1. Preheat oven to 350°F. Butter and flour a 10-inch springform pan. Set aside.
2. Beat egg yolks and sugar until fluffy (about 5 minutes). Mix in flour. Beat egg whites until stiff. Fold in batter. Pour into prepared pan and bake in preheated 350°F. oven until skewer inserted comes out clean (about 30 minutes). Remove from oven to cool on wire rack.
3. Prepare Marzipan Filling and set aside.
4. Prepare Whipped Cream Frosting and refrigerate.
5. When cake is cool, remove from pan and slice into three layers. Cover bottom layer with Whipped Cream Frosting. Place second layer over whipped cream. Cover with raspberry jam and sprinkle with orange liqueur.
6. Dust the bottom disc of a 10-inch springform pan with sugar. Place the marzipan in the center of the disc and, with a rolling pin, roll marzipan into a thin circle. With a sharp knife, trim excess marzipan from around the edge of the disc.
7. Invert the springform disc with the marzipan over the sec-

ond cake layer. With a long metal spatula, gently loosen the marzipan onto the cake. Top with the third cake layer. Frost top and sides of cake with remaining Whipped Cream Frosting. If desired, reserve some frosting to make whipped cream rosettes. To serve, cut into 16 wedges.

Marzipan Filling

1 cup almond paste
1 egg white
1½ cups confectioners' sugar

Crumble almond paste into a mixing bowl or the workbowl of a food processor fitted with a steel blade. Mix or process almond paste with egg whites until smooth. Gradually add sugar and beat or process until smooth. (If mixture is too thick to work with a mixer, it can be mixed by hand.)

Whipped Cream Frosting

2 cups whipping cream
½ cup confectioners' sugar
Peel of 1 orange, grated
3 tablespoons orange liqueur

Whip cream until soft peaks form. Gradually add sugar, while continuing to beat, until soft peaks form. Mix in orange peel and orange liqueur. Taste and add more liqueur if desired.

Salzburger Cake
(Salzburger Torte)

MAKES 16 SERVINGS

My experimentation with some favorite ingredients, like chocolate, almonds, and chestnut puree, created this exquisite cake—a cake so special it can carry the name of the jewel-box town of Salzburg.

7 eggs, separated
¾ cup sugar
1½ cups almonds, ground
⅓ cup semisweet chocolate morsels, ground
3 tablespoons flour
Chestnut Filling (recipe follows)

Garnish
½ cup slivered almonds, toasted*

1. Preheat oven to 350°F. Butter and flour a 10-inch springform pan. Set aside.
2. Beat egg yolks and sugar until light and fluffy (about 5 minutes). Mix in almonds, chocolate, and flour. Set aside. Beat egg whites until stiff. Fold in batter. Pour into prepared pan and bake in preheated 350°F. oven until skewer inserted comes out clean (about 35 minutes). Remove from oven to cool on wire rack.
3. Prepare Chestnut Filling and set aside to cool.
4. When cake is cool, slice into two layers. Frost bottom layer with Chestnut Filling. Top with second layer and frost top and sides with remaining filling. Place a 4-inch-wide jar lid or other round form over center of cake. Sprinkle toasted

---

*To toast almonds: Place almonds on a cookie sheet in preheated 350°F. oven or in a heavy skillet on the stove over medium-high heat. Toast, tossing occasionally, until almonds are golden (about 10 to 12 minutes). Remove from heat to cool.

almond slivers over top of cake. Remove lid. To serve, cut into 16 wedges.

Chestnut Filling

>   4 egg yolks
>   ¼ cup whipping cream
>   2 tablespoons cornstarch
>   1 17½-ounce can chestnut puree (*crème de marrons vanillée*)
>   1 cup butter, at room temperature
>   ¼ cup confectioners' sugar
>   3 tablespoons rum

1. In a nonstick pan, cook egg yolks, cream, cornstarch, and chestnut puree over low heat. Stir constantly until mixture thickens. Remove from heat right away. Set aside to cool.
2. Beat butter and sugar until light and fluffy. Add cooled chestnut mixture and beat until smooth. Taste and add more sugar or rum if desired.

Eggwhite Chocolate Cake
(Eiweiss Blitz Torte)

MAKES 18 SERVINGS

This wonderful cake batter takes only 10 minutes to make. As one of my "old reliables," I often include it on my dessert buffets cut into small pieces and served as petits fours (see Chapter 6).

1 cup semisweet chocolate morsels
½ cup plus 2 tablespoons butter or margarine, cut into pieces
1 cup sugar
1 cup flour
1 cup egg whites (about 6 to 8 eggs)
1 recipe Chocolate Icing (see Index)

Garnish
  Slivered almonds

Optional garnish
  1 cup whipping cream whipped with 2 tablespoons confectioners' sugar

1. Preheat oven to 350°F. Butter and flour a 10" × 4½" × 1¾" fluted cake pan (Bischofsbrot pan). Set aside.
2. Melt chocolate and butter in a heavy saucepan over low heat. Stir to combine, then set aside to cool slightly. Beat chocolate and butter with sugar and flour. Set aside. Beat egg whites until stiff. Gently mix chocolate batter into egg whites. Pour into prepared pan and bake in preheated 350°F. oven until skewer inserted in center comes out clean (about 55 to 60 minutes). Remove cake from oven and cool slightly in pan. Turn cake onto a wire rack to cool.
3. When cool, cake can be tightly wrapped and refrigerated for several days or frozen for up to 6 months. To serve, cover with Chocolate Icing and decorate with slivered almonds. If desired, garnish with sweetened whipped cream. Cut into 18 slices.

Eggwhite Almond Layer Cake
(*Eiweiss Mandel Torte*)   MAKES 16 SERVINGS

This cake is quick, easy, and light. It makes a fabulous summer dessert.

1 cup egg whites (about 6 to 8 eggs)
1 cup sugar
2 cups almonds, ground
1 cup flour
1 recipe desired buttercream (see Chapter 9)

1. Preheat oven to 275° F. Butter and flour two 10-inch spring-form pans. Set aside.
2. Beat egg whites until stiff. Combine remaining ingredients, except buttercream, in another bowl. Fold in beaten whites and pour batter into prepared pans. Bake in preheated 275° F. oven until inserted skewer comes out clean (about 15 to 20 minutes). Remove to wire rack to cool.
3. Remove cakes from pans. Prepare buttercream and frost bottom layer with buttercream. Top with remaining layer and frost top and sides with buttercream. To serve, cut into 16 wedges.

Variation

Eggwhite Almond Layer Cake (preceding recipe)
¼ cup raspberry jam
1 cup whipping cream
2 tablespoons confectioners' sugar

1. Prepare cake through Step 2 of basic recipe.
2. When cakes are cool, remove from pans. Spread raspberry jam on bottom layer. Top with remaining layer. Whip cream until soft peaks form. Continue whipping, while gradually adding sugar, until stiff peaks form. Frost top and sides of cake with whipped cream. To serve, cut into 16 wedges.

Chocolate Walnut Cake with Whipped Cream
(Schokoladen Nuss Torte mit Schlagobers)   MAKES 16 SERVINGS

You can never have too many chocolate cake recipes—this version is especially good and moist from the ground walnuts in the batter.

1 cup semisweet chocolate morsels
6 eggs, separated
⅓ cup sugar
1½ cups walnuts, ground
1 teaspoon instant coffee dissolved in 1 tablespoon water
3 tablespoons flour
1 cup whipping cream
2 tablespoons confectioners' sugar
¼ cup apricot jam

1.   Preheat oven to 350°F. Butter and flour a 10-inch springform pan. Melt chocolate and set aside.
2.   Beat egg yolks and sugar until light and fluffy (about 3 minutes). Mix in walnuts, coffee, chocolate, and flour. Set aside. Beat egg whites until stiff. Fold into batter and pour into prepared baking pan. Bake in preheated 350°F. oven until skewer inserted in center comes out clean (about 35 minutes). Remove to wire rack to cool.
3.   Whip cream until soft peaks form. Continue whipping, while gradually adding sugar, until stiff peaks form. Remove cake from pan and slice into two layers. Frost bottom layer with apricot jam. Top with other layer. Frost top and sides with whipped cream. To serve, cut into 16 wedges.

Walnut Coffeecream Torte
(Nusstorte mit Kaffeecreme)   MAKES 16 SERVINGS

This elegant cake is really very easy to make—and it's a cake you can bake on the spur of the moment. If you keep walnuts and cake crumbs in the freezer, you won't have to do any shopping because all the ingredients will be in your pantry.

8 eggs, separated
1 cup sugar
2 cups walnuts, ground
3 tablespoons cake, cookie, or bread crumbs
Coffee Buttercream (see Index)

Optional garnish
16 walnut halves

1. Preheat oven to 350°F. Butter and flour a 10-inch springform pan. Set aside.
2. Beat egg yolks and sugar until light and fluffy. Mix in walnuts and cake crumbs. Set aside. Beat egg whites until stiff. Fold into reserved batter and pour into prepared baking pan. Bake in preheated 350°F. oven until skewer inserted comes out clean (about 1 hour). Remove to wire rack to cool.
3. While cake cools, prepare Coffee Buttercream. Set aside to cool.
4. Remove cake from pan and cut into two layers. Frost bottom with buttercream. Top with other layer. Frost top and sides of cake with buttercream. Garnish with 16 walnut halves if desired. To serve, cut into 16 wedges.

Chocolate Chestnut Marzipan Delight
(Festliche Schokoladen Marzipan Torte)   MAKES 16 SERVINGS

I made the recipe for the basic chocolate cake rather plain so that the rich flavors of Chestnut Filling, Chocolate Icing, apricot jam, and marzipan would be the stars of this festive dessert.

5 eggs
½ cup sugar
½ cup flour
1 teaspoon baking powder
2 tablespoons "Dutch process" cocoa
1 recipe Chocolate Icing (see Index)
Chestnut Filling (recipe follows)
¼ cup apricot jam
1 cup almond paste

1.   Preheat oven to 350° F. Butter and flour a 9-inch springform pan. Set aside.
2.   Beat eggs, sugar, flour, baking powder, and cocoa until smooth. Pour batter into prepared pan and bake in preheated 350° F. oven until skewer inserted comes out clean (about 25 minutes). Remove from oven to cool on wire rack.
3.   Prepare icing and set aside to cool. Prepare Chestnut Filling and set aside to cool.
4.   When cake is cool, remove from pan and cut into two layers. Frost bottom layer with Chestnut Filling. Top with remaining cake layer. Warm the apricot jam and spread on top of cake.
5.   Dust the bottom disc of a springform pan with sugar. Place the almond paste in the center of the disc and, with a rolling pin, roll into a thin circle. With a sharp knife, trim excess paste around edge of disc. Reserve almond paste scraps for decoration.

6. Invert the springform disc with the almond paste over the cake top. With a long metal spatula, gently loosen the almond paste onto the cake top.

7. Cover the cake top and sides with the chocolate icing. Divide almond paste scraps into 16 pieces. Roll gently between palms to form tiny balls. Decorate the outer edge of the cake with the 16 balls. To serve, cut into 16 wedges.

Chestnut Filling

1 cup chestnut puree (*crème de marrons vanillée*)
1 tablespoon lemon juice
⅓ cup whipping cream
1 egg yolk

Combine ingredients in a nonstick pan and cook over low heat until mixture thickens. Stir constantly while cooking. Remove from heat and cool.

Two-Tone Cake
(Zwei-Farben Torte)

MAKES 16 SERVINGS

Two-Tone Cake was my Tante Leona's favorite pastry recipe. It looks intricate—a yellow layer and a chocolate hazelnut layer filled with buttercream—so don't tell your guests how simple it is to make.

6 eggs, separated
⅓ cup sugar
⅓ cup flour
Peel of ½ lemon, grated
Chocolate Hazelnut Cake (recipe follows)
1 recipe Coffee or Chocolate Buttercream (see Index)
1 cup whipping cream
2 tablespoons confectioners' sugar

Garnish
    Chocolate sprinkles

1. Preheat oven to 350°F. Butter and flour a 10-inch springform pan. Set aside.
2. Beat egg yolks and sugar until light and fluffy. Mix in flour and lemon peel. Set aside. Beat egg whites until stiff and fold into reserved batter. Pour into prepared pan and bake in preheated 350°F. oven until skewer inserted comes out clean (about 15 to 20 minutes). Remove cake from oven to cool on wire rack.
3. Prepare Chocolate Hazelnut Cake. Make desired buttercream and set aside to cool. Whip cream until soft peaks form. Continue whipping, while adding sugar gradually, until stiff peaks form.
4. To assemble cake: Cut white cake into two layers. Place one layer on serving dish. Spread with buttercream. Top with Chocolate Hazelnut Cake and spread with buttercream. Top

with remaining white cake layer. Frost sides and top of cake with whipped cream. Hold a glass or other round form over center of cake. Cover cake top with chocolate sprinkles. Remove glass. To serve, cut into 16 wedges.

Chocolate Hazelnut Cake

  1 cup peeled hazelnuts, ground
  ¾ cup sugar
  1 cup semisweet chocolate morsels
  2 tablespoons flour
  6 egg whites

1. Preheat oven to 350°F. Butter and flour a 10-inch spring-form pan. Set aside.
2. Cook hazelnuts and sugar in a small, heavy saucepan over low heat until sugar melts and just coats nuts. Mixture should be golden. Remove from heat and mix in chocolate. Stir until chocolate melts. Mix in flour and set aside.
3. Beat egg whites until stiff. Fold whites into reserved chocolate-nut mixture. Pour batter into prepared pan and bake in preheated 350°F. oven until skewer inserted comes out clean (about 35 minutes). Remove from oven to cool on wire rack.

Hazelnut Cake
(Haselnusstorte)   MAKES 16 SERVINGS

Toasting the hazelnuts with the sugar really brings out the flavor of the nuts and adds a special flavor note to the cake.

1 cup peeled hazelnuts, ground
¾ cup sugar
6 eggs, separated
1 egg
⅓ cup cake crumbs
1 tablespoon flour
Hazelnut Filling (recipe follows)

1. Preheat oven to 300°F. Butter and flour a 10-inch springform pan and set aside.
2. Cook hazelnuts and 2 tablespoons sugar in a small, heavy pan over low heat. Stir constantly until sugar melts and just coats nuts. Mixture will be golden. Remove from heat and set aside to cool slightly. Beat egg yolks and the whole egg with the remaining sugar until light and fluffy (about 5 minutes). Add reserved hazelnuts, cake crumbs, and flour. Mix to combine. Set aside. Beat egg whites until stiff, then fold into reserved batter. Pour into prepared pan and bake in preheated 300°F. oven until skewer inserted in center comes out clean (about 35 minutes). Remove to wire rack to cool.
3. Prepare Hazelnut Filling and set aside to cool.
4. When cake is cool, slice into two layers. Cover bottom layer with Hazelnut Filling. Top with remaining layer and use filling to frost top and sides of cake. To serve, cut into 16 wedges.

Hazelnut Filling

3 tablespoons sugar
2 tablespoons water
3 egg yolks
3 tablespoons butter
⅓ cup peeled hazelnuts, ground and toasted
2 tablespoons rum or cognac

1. In a small, heavy saucepan, boil sugar and water. Cook until mixture reaches soft-thread stage. To test, drop a small spoonful of syrup back into the pan. If a thread forms, it is done. Remove from heat and cool for 5 minutes.
2. Mix egg yolks with syrup over low heat until thick, stirring constantly. Remove from heat and set aside.
3. Beat butter until fluffy. Mix in hazelnuts and reserved egg-sugar mixture. Mix in rum or cognac. Taste and add more liquor if desired. Set aside to cool.

Hazelnut Gâteau
(Haselnuss Schnitten)

Recently, in an exclusive pastry shop, I saw a 1-inch slice of Hazelnut Gâteau selling for $2.50! I could hardly believe my eyes. My recipe costs less than double that amount and the yield is 12 servings.

4 eggs, separated
⅓ cup sugar
⅓ cup peeled hazelnuts, ground and toasted
⅓ cup flour
Toasted Hazelnut Filling (recipe follows)

Optional garnish

12 peeled hazelnuts dipped in Chocolate Icing (see Index)

1. Preheat oven to 350°F. Line a 12″ × 4″ × 2½″ baking pan with aluminum foil. Butter and flour foil. Set aside.
2. Beat egg yolks and sugar until light and fluffy (about 5 minutes). Mix in hazelnuts and flour. Set aside. Beat egg whites until stiff. Fold whites into reserved batter. Pour into prepared pan and bake in preheated 350°F. oven until skewer inserted comes out clean (about 15 minutes). Remove from oven and turn cake onto a lightly sugared surface. Remove paper and allow to cool.
3. Prepare Toasted Hazelnut Filling and set aside to cool.
4. Trim sides of cake so they are straight. Cut cake into two layers. Cover bottom layer with Toasted Hazelnut Filling. Top with remaining layer and frost top and sides with remaining filling. If desired, dip 12 hazelnuts into Chocolate Icing and place in a line down the center of the cake. To serve, cut into 12 slices.

Toasted Hazelnut Filling

1¼ cups peeled hazelnuts, ground
¾ cup sugar
3 egg yolks
¼ cup milk
¼ cup semisweet chocolate morsels
½ cup butter, at room temperature
3 tablespoons rum

1. In a small, heavy saucepan, cook hazelnuts and sugar, stirring constantly, until sugar melts and just coats nuts. Mixture should be golden. Mix in egg yolks, milk, and chocolate. Stir constantly over low heat until chocolate melts and mixture thickens. Remove from heat and set aside to cool.
2. Beat in butter and rum. Taste and add more sugar and rum if desired.

Viennese Chocolate Cake
(Echte Wiener Schokoladentorte)

MAKES 16 SERVINGS

This chocolate cake is too good to resist—so don't even try. Light chocolate cake layers, apricot jam, buttercream, chocolate icing, and almonds—divine!

1 cup semisweet chocolate morsels
¾ cup butter or margarine, at room temperature
¾ cup sugar
8 eggs, separated
¾ cup flour
½ recipe desired buttercream (see Chapter 9)
1 recipe Chocolate Icing (see Index)
¼ cup apricot jam

Garnish
16 almond slivers

1.   Preheat oven to 350° F. Butter and flour a 10-inch springform pan and set aside.
2.   Melt chocolate and set aside. Cream butter and sugar until fluffy. Beat in egg yolks until combined. Mix in chocolate and flour and set batter aside. Beat egg whites until stiff and fold into reserved batter. Pour into prepared pan and bake in preheated 350° F. oven until skewer inserted comes out clean (about 50 to 60 minutes). Remove to wire rack to cool.
3.   Prepare desired buttercream and Chocolate Icing. Set aside to cool.
4.   Remove cake from pan. Turn cake upside down and cut into two layers. Place bottom layer on serving plate and frost with desired buttercream. Top with remaining layer and spread apricot jam over top. Cover top and sides of cake with Chocolate Icing. Decorate with almond slivers around top edge of cake. To serve, cut into 16 wedges.

5

Jam, Cheese, Fruit, and Nut Tarts

Homemade tarts are among the most satisfying pastries you can bake for family or guests. Whether the crust is topped with jam, nuts, fruit, or cheese, there's something lovingly old-fashioned and inviting about a tart.

My tart recipes include the well-known raspberry jam-filled Linzer Torte, as well as cherry, cheese, apple, plum, and walnut tarts. All of them are quick and simple to make because the basic pastry is the cookie type, tender crust. All the ingredients are simply mixed together until they form a ball, unlike the short, flaky pastry in which cold butter must be cut into the flour before liquids are added.

In this chapter I show you how easy it is to make a pretty lattice crust as the crowning glory for your special tarts.

Linzer Torte I

MAKES 16 SERVINGS

The famous Viennese Linzer Torte is actually a snap to make—you mix a pastry dough with ground almonds, cover it with jam and a lattice top, then bake it. What could be simpler? The hard part is waiting for two days after it's baked for the flavor to develop. That's what I suggest, but if you can't wait, go ahead and enjoy.

2 cups almonds, ground
1 cup butter or margarine, at room temperature
4 egg yolks
½ cup sugar
1¼ cup flour
2 tablespoons cinnamon
½ cup raspberry jam

Garnish
Confectioners' sugar

1. Preheat oven to 350° F.
2. If almonds are ground in food processor, leave them in workbowl and add remaining ingredients except jam. Process until a ball forms. If almonds are ground in a nut grinder, grind them and set aside. Combine all ingredients except almonds and jam. Add almonds and mix.
3. Pat two thirds of the dough into the bottom of a 9-inch springform pan. Spread with raspberry jam. Place remaining dough on a lightly floured board, dust lightly with flour (add enough so dough is not sticky), and cover with plastic wrap. Roll dough ⅛ inch thick. Cut into ½-inch-wide strips with a plain or fluted pastry wheel. Arrange strips in a lattice pattern on top of torte (see illustration). Press gently to attach strips to dough bottom, then trim excess.
4. Bake until lattice is golden (about 50 minutes). Remove from oven to wire rack to cool. To serve, remove from pan and dust with confectioners' sugar. Cut into 16 wedges.

Note: The torte develops more flavor if allowed to sit for two days before serving. It also keeps for up to two weeks in the refrigerator.

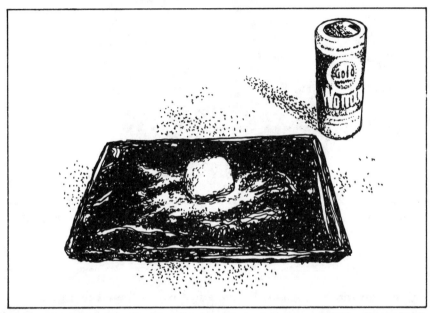

Form dough into a ball. Place on a lightly floured work surface. Sprinkle lightly with flour and cover with a sheet of plastic wrap.

Roll dough into a rectangle ⅛ inch thick. Trim sides with a fluted pastry wheel to make an even rectangle. Gather scraps into a ball and set aside. (Scraps can be frozen and used again.)

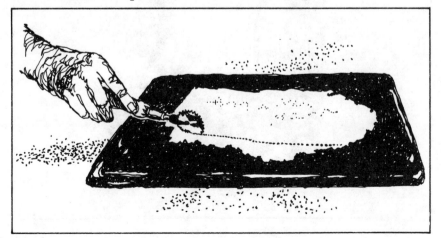

With a ruler and a pastry wheel, make a mark every ½ inch on the shorter end of the rectangle.

Cut dough into ½-inch-wide strips following the guide marks.

Dip metal spatula into flour container. Use spatula to lift each lattice strip onto top of tart. Dip spatula into flour as often as necessary. Arrange strips in a crisscross pattern.

Press down gently with fingertips to secure lattice. Press lattice strips to sides of tart to secure. Trim excess dough from strips.

Finished lattice tart.

Linzer Torte II   MAKES 16 SERVINGS

There are so many variations of the Linzer Torte that I just had to include one more recipe. This version uses whole eggs instead of egg yolks and a touch of baking powder for added lightness. A bit of cocoa in the dough adds another flavor dimension to the torte.

1½ cups almonds, ground
1 cup butter or margarine, at room temperature
4 eggs
1 cup sugar
2½ cups flour
2 tablespoons cinnamon
1 tablespoon "Dutch process" cocoa
1 teaspoon baking powder
1 cup raspberry jam

Garnish
 Confectioners' sugar

1. Preheat oven to 350° F.
2. If almonds are ground in food processor, leave them in workbowl and add remaining ingredients except jam. Process until a ball forms. If almonds are ground in a nut grinder, grind them and set aside. Combine all ingredients except almonds and jam. Add almonds and mix.
3. Pat two thirds of the dough into the bottom of a 9- or 10-inch springform pan. Spread with raspberry jam. Place remaining dough on a lightly floured board, dust lightly with flour (add enough so dough is not sticky), and cover with plastic wrap. Roll dough ⅛ inch thick. Cut into ½-inch-wide strips with a plain or fluted pastry wheel. Arrange strips in a lattice pattern on top of torte (see illustration). Press gently to attach strips to dough bottom, then trim excess.
4. Bake until lattice is golden (about 50 to 60 minutes depending on which size pan is used). Remove from oven to wire rack to cool. To serve, remove from pan and dust with confectioners' sugar. Cut into 16 wedges.

   Note: The torte develops more flavor if allowed to sit for two days before serving. It also keeps for up to two weeks in the refrigerator.

Hungarian Cheesecake Tart
(Muerber Teig)   MAKES 48 PIECES

If you're a cheesecake lover, you'll flip over this silky smooth filling with golden raisins and a touch of lemon.

Pastry Crust (recipe follows)
3 tablespoons butter, at room temperature
1 8-ounce package cream cheese, at room temperature
¼ cup sour cream
⅓ cup sugar
3 eggs, separated
Peel of 1 small or ½ large lemon, grated
¼ cup golden raisins

Garnish
   Confectioners' sugar

1.   Prepare Pastry Crust and refrigerate for 1 hour.
2.   Preheat oven to 350° F. Cream butter, cream cheese, and sour cream until smooth. Beat in sugar until smooth. Add egg yolks, one at a time, and beat until smooth. Mix in lemon peel. Set mixture aside.
3.   Divide pastry into two parts. Roll one half on a lightly floured surface into a ⅛-inch-thick rectangle. Fit pastry into a 13″ × 9″ × 2″ baking pan.
4.   Beat egg whites until stiff. Fold egg whites and raisins into reserved filling. Pour into pastry crust. Roll remaining half of pastry crust into a rectangle large enough to cover the tart. If crust is difficult to transfer in one piece, divide it into two or three pieces. Lay each piece over filling and mend together. Press edges of top and side crust to seal. Bake in preheated 350° F. oven until golden (about 20 to 25 minutes). Remove to wire rack to cool. Dust with confectioners' sugar. To serve, cut into 48 pieces.

Pastry Crust

2½ cups flour
¼ cup sugar
½ cup butter, at room temperature
⅓ cup solid vegetable shortening
3 egg yolks
2 tablespoons white wine
Peel of 1 small or ½ large lemon, grated

Combine flour and sugar. Mix in remaining ingredients to form a ball. Cover and refrigerate for 1 hour.

Open-Faced Apple Tart
(Muerber Teig)

MAKES 48 PIECES

Years ago, the sister of Mausi, my German-born hairdresser, came to visit her in Chicago. During her stay she baked an apple cake that I just loved. She was kind enough to share the recipe with me, so I'm going to share it with you. This Open-Faced Apple Tart is representative of the wonderful cooking of her hometown of Ottobeuern (near Munich), which is also famous for its beautiful baroque church.

Pastry Crust (recipe follows)
½ cup butter
½ cup sugar
3 eggs
2 tablespoons vanilla extract
Peel of 1 lemon, grated
3 pounds apples (preferably Granny Smith)
2 tablespoons cinnamon

1. Prepare Pastry Crust and refrigerate for 1 hour. Melt butter and set aside to cool.
2. Preheat oven to 300°F. Combine melted butter, sugar, eggs, vanilla, and lemon peel in a bowl. Set aside.
3. Peel and core apples. Slice ⅛ to ¼ inch thick. Set aside. Roll pastry on a lightly floured surface into a ⅛-inch-thick rectangle. Fit dough into a 15" × 10" × 1" baking pan. Trim excess dough. Place sliced apples into pan and sprinkle with cinnamon. Pour reserved filling over apples and bake in preheated 300°F. oven until golden (about 35 minutes). Remove from oven and cool on wire rack. When cool, cut into 2-inch squares. Makes about 4 dozen squares.

Pastry Crust

2½ cups flour
⅓ cup sugar
¾ cup butter, at room temperature
3 egg yolks
2 tablespoons white wine
Peel of 1 small or ½ large lemon, grated

Combine flour and sugar. Mix in remaining ingredients to form a ball. Cover and refrigerate for 1 hour.

Lattice Nut Tart
(Muerber Kuchen mit Nussfuelle)   MAKES 16 SERVINGS

My Tante Peppi, who was actually not my aunt but a dear old family friend, jealously guarded her recipes. But I loved this nut tart so much that I finally wore her down with all my pestering and got the recipe.

Pastry Crust (recipe follows)
2 cups walnuts, ground
¾ cup confectioners' sugar
3 eggs
Peel of 1 small lemon, grated
1 tablespoon rum

1.   Prepare Pastry Crust and refrigerate 1 hour.
2.   Preheat oven to 350°F.
3.   If nuts are ground in food processor, leave them in workbowl and add remaining ingredients. Process to combine. Set aside. If nuts are ground in a nut grinder, grind them and set aside. Beat remaining ingredients until well mixed. Stir in nuts. Set aside.
4.   Remove crust from refrigerator. Cut off one third of the dough and refrigerate. Press the remaining two thirds of the dough into the bottom of a 10-inch springform pan. If dough is sticky, dust lightly with flour. Pour nut filling into pan.
5.   Place remaining dough on lightly floured surface and sprinkle lightly with flour. Cover dough with plastic wrap. Roll ¼ inch thick. Cut into ½-inch-wide strips with a plain or fluted pastry wheel. Lay the strips crosswise over the tart in a lattice pattern (see illustration).
5.   Bake in preheated 350°F. oven until lattice is golden and a skewer inserted in center comes out clean (about 60 minutes). If tart is not done after 60 minutes, turn heat off and leave in oven 15 to 20 minutes more. The bottom takes longer to bake

than the top, so if lattice begins to brown too fast, cover with aluminum foil.

7. Remove from oven to cool on wire rack. To serve, cut into 16 wedges.

Pastry Crust

2½ cups flour
¾ cup butter or margarine, at room temperature
½ cup sugar
3 egg yolks
Peel of 1 small lemon, grated

In a food processor fitted with a steel blade or with electric mixer, combine all ingredients until they form a ball. Wrap and refrigerate for at least 1 hour.

Plum Tart
(Zetschkenkuchen)

MAKES 12 SERVINGS

This Plum Tart can be baked the day before serving, but it is better fresh. I like to put it in the oven about an hour before dinner. While it's baking, the aroma of the plums and cinnamon drives everyone into ecstasy. Of course, you can only enjoy this special treat at plum time, which is late summer and early fall.

  2 cups flour
  2 teaspoons baking powder
  ¼ cup butter or margarine, at room temperature
  2 eggs
  Peel of 1 lemon, grated
  1 tablespoon milk
  2 pounds Italian plums
  3 tablespoons cinnamon
  ¼ cup sugar
  3 tablespoons butter, melted
  Apricot jam

1. Preheat oven to 350°F.
2. Combine flour, baking powder, ¼ cup butter, eggs, and lemon peel. Add milk, 1 teaspoon at a time, until dough is bound together. Pat the dough into a 13″ × 9″ × 2″ baking pan. Set aside.
3. Slice plums in half and remove pits. Arrange plums, skin side down, on top of the dough. Position plums closely together and press gently into the dough. If they stick out too much, make a slit at each end of plum and press down. Mix cinnamon and sugar and sprinkle over plums. Pour a little melted butter in center of each plum. Put about ¼ teaspoon apricot jam in center of each plum.
4. Bake in preheated 350°F. oven until plums are cooked and jam forms a glaze (about 45 minutes). Let tart sit for about 15 minutes before serving. To serve, cut into 12 rectangular

pieces. Take care when cutting to cut between plums—the pieces are much prettier if the plums are kept whole.

Cherry Shortcake
(Muerber Teig mit Kirschen) MAKES 24 PIECES

For best flavor, be sure to use good quality sour cherries.

Sour Cream Pastry (recipe follows)
6 eggs, separated
1¼ cups sugar
1 cup chocolate cookie or cake crumbs
Peel of 1 orange, grated
2 16-ounce cans sour cherries, well drained *or* 1 pound
    fresh cherries, stemmed and pitted

1. Preheat oven to 350°F. Prepare Sour Cream Pastry and press into the bottom of a 13″ × 9″ × 2″ baking pan. Bake for 15 minutes.

2. While pastry is baking, mix egg yolks, sugar, cookie or cake crumbs, and orange peel together. Beat egg whites until stiff and fold into batter.

3. After pastry has baked 15 minutes, remove from oven and pour drained cherries over crust. Pour filling over top and return to oven. Bake until golden (about 10 to 15 minutes). Remove to a wire rack to cool. Cut into 24 pieces.

Sour Cream Pastry

    2 cups flour
    ⅓ cup sugar
    ½ cup butter, at room temperature
    2 egg yolks
    ¼ cup sour cream

    Combine flour and sugar. Mix in remaining ingredients to form a ball.

Apple-Raisin Tart
(Apfel Lattice Schnitten)

MAKES 30 PIECES

After experimenting with many different combinations of apples and flavorings for an original apple tart recipe, my friends and I decided that this recipe was the winner. It combines a rich sour cream crust with an apple, orange juice, lemon peel, and raisin filling. The pretty lattice crust gives it the final touch.

Sour Cream Pastry Crust (see preceding recipe)
3 pounds apples, peeled and cored (preferably Granny Smith)
¼ cup frozen orange juice concentrate, thawed
3 tablespoons apricot jam
1 tablespoon lemon peel, grated
2 tablespoons raisins
2 to 3 tablespoons confectioners' sugar (optional)
1 egg white

Garnish
Confectioners' sugar

1. Make Sour Cream Pastry Crust and refrigerate while filling cooks. Preheat oven to 350° F.
2. Cook apples in orange juice until soft. Mash apples against side of pan with the back of a large spoon. Add remaining ingredients except sugar and egg white. Taste and add 2 to 3 tablespoons confectioners' sugar, if desired. Set aside.
3. Take dough from refrigerator. Cut off one third of dough and return that piece to refrigerator. Press remaining dough into a 13″ × 9″ × 2″ baking pan. Dip palms into flour so dough does not stick. Pour apple filling into pan. Set aside.
4. Remove the dough from refrigerator and place on a lightly floured surface. Dust lightly with flour and cover with

plastic wrap. Roll dough ⅛ inch thick. Cut into ½-inch-wide lattice strips (see illustration). Arrange in a crisscross pattern on top of tart. Beat egg white with a fork, then brush lattice strips with egg white. Bake in preheated 350°F. oven until lattice is golden (about 50 to 60 minutes). Remove from oven to cool on wire rack.

5. When tart is cool, dust with confectioners' sugar. To serve, cut into 30 squares.

6

Petits Fours and Cookies

Petits fours are the shiniest jewels in the pastry maker's crown. Even the most committed dieter finds it hard to resist "just one" of these tempting morsels.

A tray of gorgeous petits fours will always raise a chorus of "Oohs" and "Aahs" from guests—a chorus that will continue after they taste. My petits fours, like Peggy Puffs, Chocolate Petits Fours, and Marzipan Dates, have the flavor to match their good looks.

My best fancy cookie recipes appear in this chapter because they fit so well on the petits fours tray. Crisp, spicy Ischler cookies are the best-known Austrian cookie and I've included three variations from one basic dough. Moist, chewy Florentine Cookies and Chocolate Nut Cookies are two of my other favorites you will find here.

None of the recipes are difficult or take as much time as you might imagine. With my recipes and decorating tips, you'll be able to create miniature pastries that look and taste so great that your friends may not believe you made them.

Chocolate Petits Fours
(Schokoladen Petits Fours)

MAKES 48 PIECES

This basic recipe offers a wonderful chance for creativity. If you have small amounts of buttercreams and icings in the freezer you can use them in this recipe to create a variety of petits fours. Use your imagination, too, to create original decorations.

1 cup semisweet chocolate morsels
6 eggs, separated
⅓ cup sugar
¾ cup butter, at room temperature
⅓ cup flour
1 recipe desired buttercream (see Chapter 9)
1 recipe desired icing (see Chapter 9)

Garnish
  Glacéed cherries
  Chocolate sprinkles

1. Preheat oven to 350°F. Line a 17″ × 12″ × 2″ baking pan with aluminum foil. Butter and flour foil. Set aside. Melt chocolate and set aside.
2. Beat egg yolks and sugar until light and fluffy (about 3 minutes). Beat in chocolate, butter, and flour. Set aside. Beat egg whites until stiff. Fold into chocolate batter and pour into prepared pan. Bake in preheated 350°F. oven until skewer inserted comes out clean (about 20 minutes). Be careful not to overbake or cake will dry out. Remove to wire rack to cool.
3. Using 1- or 1½-inch cookie cutters (in a variety of shapes like circles, triangles, etc.), cut cake into various cutouts. Make sure there are an even number of each shape because the petits fours will be sandwiched together.

4. Spread half the cutouts with buttercream (they can also be spread with jam if desired). Top with remaining cutouts. Pour or brush icing on tops with pastry brush. Decorate with quartered glacéed cherries or chocolate sprinkles. Tops can also be decorated with a decorating comb (page 7). To serve, place each petit four in a small paper cup.

Marzipan Dates
(Marzipan Datteln)   MAKES 44 PIECES

These Marzipan Dates take just minutes to make and are a pretty addition to a pastry tray. Be sure to use large dates with stones—when you take out the stone you have a cavity in which to put the delicious marzipan.

22 large dates with stones (about 1 pound)
½ cup almond paste
1 to 2 tablespoons egg white
2 teaspoons raspberry jam
Peel of ½ lemon, grated
1 to 2 drops green food coloring
1 recipe Chocolate Icing (see Index)

1. Remove stones from dates and discard them. Set dates aside. Mix remaining ingredients except Chocolate Icing. Add just enough egg white to bind mixture. Fill each date cavity with marzipan mixture. Dry in refrigerator for 30 minutes.
2. Prepare Chocolate Icing and set aside to cool.
3. Position dates so marzipan filling is on bottom. Spoon Chocolate Icing over top of dates. Return to refrigerator for 20 minutes. When chocolate is set, dates can be stored in a box or tin in the refrigerator or served right away. To serve, cut each date in half and place marzipan side up in a paper candy cup. Serve on a tray with other petits fours.

Chocolate Cake with Chocolate Whipped Cream Filling
(Rigo Jancsi)
MAKES 20 PIECES

Rigo Jancsi actually means clown, but I don't know how such a wonderful dessert got such an odd name. It's a great delicacy in Hungary, and friends who went to Budapest before the war came back to Vienna raving about it. The recipe I'm including here is one of the simplest and best tasting of any I have tried.

½ cup semisweet chocolate morsels
¾ cup butter or margarine, at room temperature
½ cup sugar
4 eggs, separated
½ cup flour
Chocolate Whipped Cream Filling (recipe follows)
½ recipe Chocolate Icing (see Index)

Optional garnish
   1 cup whipping cream whipped with 2 tablespoons
      confectioners' sugar

1. Preheat oven to 350°F. Line a 17″ × 12″ × 2″ pan with foil. Butter and flour the foil and set aside. Melt chocolate and set aside.

2. Cream butter and sugar until fluffy (about 3 minutes). Add egg yolks one at a time and beat well to combine. Mix in melted chocolate. Mix in flour and set aside. Beat egg whites until stiff. Fold whites into reserved batter and spread on prepared baking sheet. Bake in preheated 350°F. oven until cake starts to come away from sides of pan (about 15 minutes). Remove from oven to cool on wire rack.

3. While cake is cooling, prepare Chocolate Whipped Cream

Filling. Refrigerate. Prepare Chocolate Icing and set aside to cool.

4.   Cut cooled cake into 2 pieces, each 8½ × 11 inches. Cut one of the pieces into 20 rectangles. Set aside. On the remaining half, spread the Chocolate Whipped Cream Filling. Top with the reserved 20 rectangles. (By precutting the top pieces, the filling won't be squeezed out by the pressure of slicing). Spread the Chocolate Icing over the top. Allow icing to set, then slice into 20 rectangles, using the top pieces as cutting guidelines. Serve with sweetened whipped cream, if desired.

Chocolate Whipped Cream Filling

   2 cups whipping cream
   ½ cup plus 2 tablespoons confectioners' sugar
   ¼ cup "Dutch process" cocoa
   2 tablespoons rum, bourbon, or cognac

   Whip cream until soft peaks form. Continue beating, while gradually adding confectioners' sugar, until stiff peaks form. Mix in cocoa and rum.

Peggy Puffs
(Margareten Krapferln)

MAKES ABOUT 24 PIECES

These meringue petits fours with walnut cream filling and chocolate icing are named after my daughter Peggy.

6 egg whites
¾ cup sugar
1½ cups walnuts, ground
Peel of 1 small lemon, grated
Walnut Cream Filling (recipe follows)
1 recipe Chocolate Icing (see Index)

1. Preheat oven to 250° F. Butter a large baking sheet and set aside.
2. Beat egg whites until soft peaks form. Continue beating, while adding sugar, until stiff peaks form. Fold in ground walnuts and lemon peel. Drop mixture by tablespoonfuls onto the prepared baking sheet (there should be about 50 puffs). Bake in preheated 250° F. oven until golden (about 25 minutes). Remove to a wire rack to cool.
3. While puffs are cooling, prepare Walnut Cream Filling and Chocolate Icing. Set icing aside to cool.
4. Spread half the puffs with Walnut Cream Filling. Top with remaining puffs. Use a pastry brush to cover tops with Chocolate Icing.

Walnut Cream Filling

2 tablespoons butter, at room temperature
¼ cup confectioners' sugar
½ cup walnuts, ground
1 tablespoon "Dutch-process" cocoa
1 tablespoon apricot or raspberry jam

Cream butter and sugar until fluffy. Mix in remaining ingredients and beat until smooth.

Nut Chocolate Rounds
(Schwartz Weisse Nuss Ringerln)   MAKES ABOUT 30 PIECES

This is one of the quickest petits fours to make. The cookie dough, jam, and nut-chocolate topping are baked in one pan, then cut into rounds with a cookie cutter.

1 cup butter or margarine, at room temperature
¾ cup sugar
2 cups flour
Juice of ½ lemon and peel, grated
1 cup nuts, ground
1 cup semisweet chocolate morsels, ground or melted
4 egg whites
1 cup confectioners' sugar
½ cup apricot or raspberry jam

1. Preheat oven to 350°F.
2. Mix butter, ¾ cup sugar, flour, lemon juice, and peel until combined. Press into a 15″ × 10″ × 1½″ baking pan. Set aside.
3. If grinding nuts and chocolate in food processor, grind separately, then combine with remaining ingredients except jam. Process until smooth. If nuts and chocolate are ground in a nut grinder, grind and set aside. Beat egg whites with 1 cup confectioners' sugar until smooth. Mix in nuts and chocolate. Set aside.
4. Spread jam over dough in reserved pan. Pour topping over jam. Bake in preheated 350°F. oven until golden (about 45 minutes). Remove to wire rack to cool.
5. When lukewarm, cut into 1½-inch rounds with a cookie cutter. Dip the cutter occasionally in warm water to clean it. (These can also be sliced into 2″ × 1″ rectangles.)

Ischler Cookies
(Ischler Krapfen)

MAKES ABOUT 88 PIECES

Ischler Cookies take their name from the charming little town of Ischl (near Salzburg), which was the summer residence of Emperor Franz Josef. The Emperor was very fond of these spicy cookies. My good friend, Dick, who's not an emperor but has the taste of one, loves them too.

2 cups almonds, ground
1¼ cups butter or margarine, at room temperature
⅔ cup sugar
2 cups flour
2 tablespoons cinnamon, or more to taste (use half
    allspice if desired)
Apricot jam
1 recipe Chocolate Icing (see Index)

Garnish
  Slivered almonds

1.   If almonds are ground in food processor, leave them in workbowl and add butter, sugar, flour, and cinnamon. Process until mixed. If almonds are ground in a nut grinder, grind them and set aside. Cream butter and sugar until fluffy. Mix in flour, cinnamon, and almonds. Mix to combine. If necessary, finish mixing dough with hands. If dough is sticky, add a couple of tablespoons flour. If dough is too dry, add 1 to 2 tablespoons water or coffee. Wrap dough well and chill for at least 1 hour.

2.   Preheat oven to 350°F.

3.   Divide dough into three parts. Refrigerate remaining dough while rolling each piece. Lightly flour a work surface and place dough in center. Sprinkle dough lightly with flour and cover with plastic wrap. Roll ¼ inch thick. Cut into rounds (sizes specified below) and place on an ungreased cookie sheet. Bake in preheated 350°F. oven until cookies feel firm to the touch (about 12 minutes). Remove to wire rack to

cool. Roll remaining two pieces of dough; cut and decorate as indicated below and in illustration.

4. *First piece of dough:* Cut rolled dough into 1½-inch rounds; bake and cool. Spread half the cookies with ½ teaspoon apricot jam. Top with remaining cookies. Spoon or brush Chocolate Icing over sandwiches. Decorate with slivered almonds. Makes 22 sandwiches.

5. *Second piece of dough:* Cut rolled dough into 2-inch rounds; bake and cool. Dip half of each cookie into Chocolate Icing. Place on wire rack until chocolate sets. Makes 44 cookies.

6. *Third piece of dough:* Cut rolled dough into 2-inch rounds. With half of cookies, use a 1-inch or ½-inch round cutter to make cutouts in center. Remove cutouts and bake with remaining cookies. When cookies are cool, make sandwiches with the whole cookies and the cookie rings, using apricot jam in center. Use jam to "glue" cutouts around top of sandwiches for decoration. Decorate with Chocolate Icing and almond slivers. Makes 22 sandwiches.

First variation: Second and third cookies from left in the top row are sandwich cookies covered with Chocolate Icing and decorated with a slivered almond. *Second variation:* First two cookies from right in the top row are single cookies half dipped in Chocolate Icing. *Third variation:* Some of remaining cookies are sandwiches made with one solid cookie and one ring cookie decorated with Chocolate Icing, chocolate sprinkles, jam, or almonds. Some are solid cookies covered with jam and decorated with round cookie cutouts, icing, almonds, and sprinkles.

Marzipan Ischler Tarts
(Marzipan Ischler Krapfen)
MAKES ABOUT 60 TARTS

Ischler Cookies (preceding recipe)
Raspberry jam
1 cup almond paste
1 recipe Chocolate Icing (see Index)

Garnish
Slivered almonds

1. Prepare Ischler dough; chill, roll, and cut into 1½-inch rounds. Bake according to recipe instructions in Step 3. Remove to wire rack to cool.
2. Spread half the cookies with raspberry jam.
3. Dust work surface lightly with confectioners' sugar. Place almond paste in center. Cover with plastic wrap and roll ⅛ inch thick. Cut into 1½-inch rounds and place on top of jam-covered cookies. Spread marzipan lightly with raspberry jam and cover with remaining cookies. Spoon or brush Chocolate Icing over tops. Garnish each tart with a slivered almond.

Tony's Hussar Cookies
(Husarenkrapferl)
MAKES ABOUT 30 COOKIES

Hussar Cookies, coated with almonds and topped with jam, were always a favorite of my son Tony. These delicate butter cookies keep well in a tin, but don't garnish them with jam until just before serving—they'll stay prettier that way.

½ cup butter or margarine, at room temperature
⅓ cup sugar
2 egg yolks
1¼ cups flour
Peel of 1 lemon, grated
1 egg white
½ cup slivered almonds, lightly crushed

Garnish
   3 tablespoons raspberry jam

1. Cream butter and sugar. Add egg yolks and beat. Mix in flour and lemon peel. Cover and refrigerate for 1 hour.
2. Preheat oven to 350°F. Line a baking sheet with aluminum foil and butter lightly. Set aside.
3. Roll cookie dough between palms into walnut-size balls and place about 1 inch apart on the prepared baking sheet. If you want cookies precisely the same size, use your palms to roll all the dough into a sausage shape about 1 inch in diameter. Cut into ½-inch pieces; roll each piece into a ball. Dip index finger into flour; press an indentation in the center of each cookie with index finger. Brush tops of cookies with egg white, then dip into crushed almonds. Bake in preheated 350°F. oven until golden (about 12 to 15 minutes). Cool on wire rack.
4. When cookies cool, fill center of each cookie with about ¼ teaspoon of jam.

Variation: Chocolate Hussar Cookies

Tony's Hussar Cookies (preceding recipe)
¼ cup semisweet chocolate morsels, melted
2 tablespoons flour

Garnish
   1½ tablespoons apricot jam

Prepare dough as in Step 1 of basic recipe. Divide dough in half. Prepare half as in basic recipe. Mix melted chocolate and 2 tablespoons flour into other half of the dough. Combine both halves of dough. Do not mix completely, but leave some white streaks in the dough. Finish cookies as in preceding recipe, but substitute apricot jam for raspberry.

Chocolate Nut Cookies
(Schokolade-Nuss Pusserln)

MAKES ABOUT 72 COOKIES

This is one of the simplest, best-tasting cookie recipes you'll ever find. The cookies are light, but with a very intense, rich chocolate flavor. Wonderful!

4 egg whites
1 cup confectioners' sugar
2½ cups walnuts, ground
1½ cups semisweet chocolate morsels, ground
¼ cup flour

Garnish
Confectioners' sugar

Optional garnish
Candied cherries or pineapple, cut into small pieces

1. Beat egg whites until soft peaks form. Continue beating, while gradually adding ½ cup of confectioners' sugar, until stiff peaks form. Fold remaining sugar, nuts, chocolate, and flour into egg whites. Cover and refrigerate for 24 hours.*
2. Preheat oven to 350°F. Line a baking sheet with aluminum foil and butter lightly.
3. Using two spoons, or the palms of the hands, shape the dough into nut-size balls. Place about 1 inch apart on the prepared baking sheet. If desired, press a piece of candied cherry or pineapple onto the top of each cookie. Bake in preheated 350°F. oven until outside of cookie forms a thin shell (about 15 minutes). Remove to a wire rack to cool. Sprinkle with confectioners' sugar.

---

*If cookie dough cannot be chilled for 24 hours, prepare dough and spoon onto cookie sheet. Chill for 15 minutes before baking.

Florentine Cookies
(Florentiner)
MAKES ABOUT 48 COOKIES

These moist, chewy cookies are a Christmas favorite in Vienna.

2 eggs
1¼ cups confectioners' sugar
⅓ cup flour
1 scant teaspoon baking powder
1 scant teaspoon cinnamon
½ cup candied orange peel or glacéed mixed fruit
Peel of 1 lemon, grated
2 cups slivered almonds
3 egg whites
1 recipe Chocolate Icing (see Index)

1. Preheat oven to 300°F. Cover a baking sheet with foil and butter the foil. Set aside.
2. Beat eggs and sugar until light and fluffy (about 5 minutes). Set aside. Mix flour, baking powder, and cinnamon. Toss with candied fruit, lemon peel, and almonds. Mix with eggs and sugar; set aside. Beat egg whites until stiff. Fold egg whites into fruit and nut batter. Drop batter by scant teaspoonfuls about 1 inch apart on prepared baking sheet. Bake in preheated 300°F. oven until golden (about 10 minutes). Remove cookies to a wire rack to cool. Repeat until all cookies are baked.
3. When cookies are cool, use a pastry brush to coat tops with Chocolate Icing.

Walnut Filled Cookies
(Nusspusserln)
MAKES 60 COOKIES

This combination of rich walnut cookies and coffee icing is irresistible. For a special presentation, garnish each cookie with a walnut half.

½ cup plus 2 tablespoons butter or margarine, at room
   temperature
¼ cup sugar
2 eggs
2 cups flour
Peel of ½ lemon, grated
Nut Filling (recipe follows)
1 recipe Coffee Icing (see Index)

Optional Garnish
   60 walnut halves

1. Cream butter and sugar. Beat in eggs one at a time. Add flour and lemon peel. Mix well to combine. Wrap dough in plastic wrap and refrigerate for at least 1 hour or overnight.
2. Preheat oven to 350°F. Divide chilled dough in half; refrigerate one piece while rolling the other. Place dough on lightly floured surface and sprinkle lightly with flour. Cover dough with plastic wrap. Roll ⅛ inch thick. Cut into rounds with 1½-inch cookie cutter and place on an ungreased baking sheet. Bake in preheated 350°F. oven until cookies are golden (about 10 minutes). Repeat with second half of dough. After cookies are baked, remove to wire rack to cool.
3. Make Nut Filling and set aside. Make Coffee Icing and set aside.
4. When cookies are cool, spread ½ teaspoon of filling on half the cookies. Top with remaining cookies to make sandwiches. Spoon or brush Coffee Icing over tops of cookies and decorate with walnut halves, if desired.

Nut Filling

1 cup walnuts, ground
¼ cup butter, at room temperature
¼ cup confectioners' sugar
1 egg
1 tablespoon rum
Peel of ½ lemon, grated

If nuts are ground in food processor, leave them in workbowl. Add remaining ingredients and process until combined. If nuts are ground in a nut grinder, mix them by hand, or with an electric mixer, with remaining ingredients.

7

Coffee Cakes and Quick Breads

Coffee cakes and quick breads represent home baking at its very finest. Not terribly fancy, just delicious and downright satisfying. These kinds of pastries are perfect companions for a steaming cup of morning coffee or leisurely afternoon tea. In Vienna, they were just the thing to enjoy during *Jause,* the afternoon coffee break.

The coffee cakes—Viennese Bundt Coffee Cake, Sour Cream Coffee Cake, Walnut Strudel, and Poppy Seed Strudel—and the quick breads—Honey Bread and Bishop's Cake—all freeze beautifully. If you bake and freeze a variety of these delicious pastries, you will always be prepared for an impromptu brunch or tea party.

Viennese Bundt Coffee Cake
(Kugelhupf)
MAKES 16 SERVINGS

This Kugelhupf is doubly light—from yeast and beaten egg whites in the batter. I have included two versions: the first flavored with lemon peel and golden raisins, the second with cinnamon and walnuts.

¼ cup warm milk (80° F. to 90° F.)
1 tablespoon sugar
3 tablespoons flour
1 ounce compressed yeast, crumbled
½ cup butter or margarine, at room temperature
½ cup sugar
Peel of 2 lemons, grated
5 eggs, separated
⅓ cup whipping cream *or* half-and-half
3 cups flour
½ cup golden raisins

Garnish
Confectioners' sugar

1. Butter and flour a 10-inch bundt cake pan. Set aside.
2. In a small bowl mix the milk, 1 tablespoon sugar, 3 table-spoons flour, and the yeast. Set aside until bubbles rise to the surface (about 15 minutes).
3. In the meantime, cream butter and ½ cup sugar. Add lemon peel, egg yolks, and whipping cream. Mix well. Mix ¼ cup flour with the raisins and set aside. Pour remaining 2¾ cups flour into batter. Mix well to combine. Fold in raisins. Set batter aside. Beat 3 egg whites (save remaining 2 egg whites for another recipe) until stiff. Fold into reserved batter and pour into prepared bundt pan. Cover and set in a draft-free spot to rise until batter reaches top of pan (about 1 hour).

4.   Fifteen minutes before baking, preheat oven to 350°F. Bake cake until skewer inserted in center comes out clean (about 50 minutes). Remove cake from oven to cool on wire rack. To serve, remove cake from pan and garnish with confectioners' sugar. Cut into 16 pieces.

Variation: Cinnamon Coffee Cake (Zimtkugelhupf)

Viennese Bundt Coffee Cake (preceding recipe)
2 tablespoons cinnamon
2 tablespoons sugar
2 tablespoons walnuts, chopped

Prepare Viennese Bundt Coffee Cake batter. Pour half into bundt pan. Combine cinnamon, sugar, and nuts and sprinkle over batter. Cover with remaining batter; cover and set aside to rise for 1 hour. Bake as in Step 4 of basic recipe.

Sour Cream Coffee Cake
(Backpulverkuchen mit Rahm)
MAKES 16 SERVINGS

If you're pressed for time, you don't have to beat the egg whites separately. Add the whole eggs where the egg yolks are added in Step 2 and continue with the recipe. The results will be a denser cake with the same delicious, sour cream flavor and surprise center.

Chocolate Filling (recipe follows)
½ cup butter or margarine, at room temperature
⅔ cup sugar
4 eggs, separated
2 cups flour
2 teaspoons baking powder
1 cup sour cream
Peel of 1 lemon, grated

Garnish
Confectioners' sugar

1. Preheat oven to 350°F. Butter and flour a 10-inch bundt cake pan. Set aside. Prepare Chocolate Filling and set aside.

2. Cream butter and sugar until light and fluffy (about 3 minutes). Add egg yolks and mix to combine. Mix flour and baking powder; add to batter and mix. Mix in sour cream and lemon peel. Set aside. Beat egg whites until stiff; fold into cake batter. Pour half of batter into prepared bundt pan. Sprinkle reserved Chocolate Filling over batter and pour remaining batter over top. Bake in preheated 350°F. oven until skewer inserted in center comes out clean (about 1 hour). Remove to wire rack to cool. Remove from pan and dust cake with confectioners' sugar. To serve, cut into 16 wedges.

Chocolate Filling

> 3 tablespoons butter, at room temperature
> ½ cup semisweet chocolate morsels (preferably tiny
>   ones)
> ¼ cup confectioners' sugar
> 2 tablespoons flour
> 1 teaspoon cinnamon

Combine all ingredients and mix (mixture will be crumbly). Set aside.

Walnut and Poppy Seed Crescents
(Nuss und Mohn Kipferln)   MAKES ABOUT 48 CRESCENTS

> Walnut Strudel dough (see Index)
> Walnut Filling (see Index) *or* Poppy Seed Filling (see
>   Index) *or* ½ recipe of each

1. Prepare dough through Step 1 of basic recipe.
2. Punch dough down and divide into four parts. On a lightly floured surface, roll one piece of dough into a ⅛-inch-thick rectangle. Cut dough into squares (about 2″ × 2″). Place about 1½ teaspoons of Walnut or Poppy Seed Filling in center of each square. Starting with a pointed end, roll each square into a crescent. Pinch ends to seal. Place crescents on baking sheet. Repeat with remaining three pieces of dough.
3. Cover crescents and set in a draft-free spot to rise for 30 minutes.
4. Bake and garnish as in Step 4 of basic recipe.

Walnut Strudel
(Nuss Strudel)

MAKES 4 ROLLS

These strudels should be enjoyed at their peak of freshness—no later than 24 hours after baking. The fresh quality of the yeast dough is at its best right after the rolls cool. Of course, like all my quick breads and coffee cakes, these rolls will freeze beautifully.

I've written separate recipes for the Walnut Strudel and Poppy Seed Strudel, but if you want to sample two of each, simply cut both filling recipes in half and make two Walnut Strudels and two Poppy Seed Strudels. If you like, you can also make half the dough into rolls and half into crescents, instead of a whole recipe of either.

2 envelopes dry yeast
¼ cup lukewarm water (110°F. to 115°F.)
3 cups flour
2 tablespoons sugar
1 cup butter or margarine, at room temperature
1 egg
3 egg yolks (reserve 1 egg white for glaze)
Nut Filling (recipe follows)

Garnish
  Confectioners' sugar

1.   Dissolve yeast in lukewarm water. Mix in 1 tablespoon flour and 1 tablespoon sugar. Set aside until mixture is bubbly and doubled in bulk. Add remaining sugar, butter, the whole egg, and egg yolks. Beat to combine. Add remaining flour and mix. Turn dough onto a lightly floured work surface; knead, adding flour if dough sticks to work surface, until dough is smooth and elastic (about 10 minutes). Place dough in a greased bowl, cover, and set in a draft-free spot to rise. Let dough rise until double in bulk (about 1 hour).

2. Make Nut Filling. Put in refrigerator to cool.

3. Punch dough down and divide into four parts. On a lightly floured surface roll one piece of dough into a ⅛-inch-thick circle. Spread ¼ of the Nut Filling over dough, leaving a ½-inch border. Roll the dough, jelly-roll fashion. Pinch down length of roll to seal dough. Pinch ends to seal. Place roll, seam side down, on a baking sheet. Repeat with remaining three pieces of dough. Cover rolls and let rise in a draft-free spot for 30 minutes.

4. Fifteen minutes before baking, preheat oven to 350°F. Brush surface of rolls lightly with egg white, then bake in preheated oven until golden (about 20 to 25 minutes). Remove to wire rack to cool. Garnish with confectioners' sugar. To serve, cut into ½-inch slices.

Nut Filling

2⅔ cups walnuts, ground
1⅓ cups sugar
Peel of 1 lemon, grated
½ cup milk
2 tablespoons rum
⅓ cup raisins

Combine ingredients in a heavy pan and cook over medium heat, stirring often, until mixture bubbles and thickens. Remove from heat and cool in refrigerator.

Poppy Seed Strudel
(Mohn Strudel)

MAKES 4 ROLLS

Prepare and bake strudel as in recipe for Walnut Strudel, substituting Poppy Seed Filling (recipe follows) for Nut Filling.

Poppy Seed Filling

1 12½-ounce can poppy seed filling
¼ cup raisins
2 tablespoons rum

Mix ingredients together to combine.

Honey Bread
(Honigbrot)

This is an inexpensive cake that keeps for weeks in the refrigerator. It's especially nice as a winter treat around the holidays and it's my annual Christmas gift to my good friends Adrienne and Hans.

1 cup honey, preferably dark
2 teaspoons cinnamon
1 teaspoon nutmeg
½ cup butter or margarine
1 cup sugar
6 eggs separated
⅓ cup milk
Peel of 1 lemon, grated
Peel of 1 orange, grated
2 cups flour
2 teaspoons baking soda
1 teaspoon baking powder

1. Preheat oven to 350° F. Butter and flour a 12″ × 4″ × 2½″ loaf pan. Set aside.
2. Cook honey with spices until mixture boils. Remove from heat and set aside to cool.
3. Cream butter and sugar until fluffy. Mix in egg yolks, milk, and citrus peels until well combined. Mix flour with baking soda and baking powder. Mix into batter. Add honey and spices and mix well. Set aside. Beat egg whites until stiff. Fold into batter. Pour into prepared loaf pan and bake in preheated 350° F. oven until skewer inserted in center comes out clean (about 1 hour). Cool on a wire rack. When cake is cool, wrap and refrigerate for several days before cutting. To serve, cut into 16 slices.

Bishop's Cake
(Bischofsbrot)

MAKES 16 SERVINGS

Bishop's Cake is a light, golden cake bursting with chocolate morsels, golden raisins, and walnuts.

6 eggs, separated
½ cup sugar
1 cup flour
Peel of ½ lemon, grated
½ cup semisweet chocolate morsels
½ cup golden raisins
½ cup walnuts, chopped

1. Preheat oven to 350°F.
2. Generously butter and flour a 10″ × 4½″ × 1¾″ fluted cake pan (Bischofsbrot pan). Set aside.
3. Beat egg yolks and sugar until fluffy (about 3 minutes). Mix remaining ingredients, except egg whites, into the batter by hand. Set aside. Beat egg whites until stiff. Fold reserved batter into beaten egg whites. Pour mixture into prepared pan and bake in preheated 350°F. oven until skewer inserted in center comes out clean (about 40 minutes). Remove to wire rack to cool. To serve, remove cake from pan and cut into 16 slices.

8

Other Desserts

The desserts in this chapter have only one thing in common—great taste! For years they have delighted my family and friends, so I had to include them in the book. The only problem was the desserts were so diverse that they didn't fit into any of the other pastry categories. So, I created this "Other Desserts" chapter.

Here you'll find recipes for cold desserts like my marvelous Chocolate Raspberry Soufflé and Cream Puffs with three whipped cream fillings: coffee, chestnut, and banana. The hot desserts include a Steamed Chocolate Pudding, which is more like a soufflé than a pudding. From one basic Palatschinken (Austrian crepes) batter I have created three desserts, including an elegant Crepe Gâteau with Almond Filling. And you may never make bread pudding again once you taste my grandmother's Nussnudeln (Baked Noodle Dessert).

Cold Chocolate Raspberry Soufflé
(Kalter Schokoladen Himbeer Pudding)   MAKES 10 SERVINGS

This dessert makes a striking presentation. The tart raspberry layer is the ideal contrast to the smooth, dark chocolate.

3 tablespoons cold water
1 tablespoon unflavored gelatin
2 eggs, separated
¼ cup plus 2 tablespoons sugar
1 cup whipping cream
½ cup semisweet chocolate morsels
1 tablespoon bourbon
Raspberry Layer (recipe follows)

Garnish

1 cup whipping cream whipped with 2 tablespoons
confectioners' sugar

1. Pour water over gelatin in a small bowl. Set aside to soften. In a heavy saucepan, combine gelatin with egg yolks, ¼ cup sugar, and whipping cream. Cook, stirring constantly with a wooden spoon, until mixture thickens slightly (about 4 minutes). Remove from heat. Add chocolate and bourbon. Mix until chocolate melts. Set aside to cool.

2. Beat egg whites until soft peaks form. Gradually add remaining 2 tablespoons sugar, while continuing to beat, until stiff peaks form. Fold egg whites into chocolate mixture. Pour into a 5-cup ring mold or soufflé dish and refrigerate to thicken slightly (about 30 minutes).

3. Prepare Raspberry Layer and set aside to cool.

4. After chocolate layer has chilled for 30 minutes, pour raspberry soufflé mixture over top. Cover and return to refrigerator until firm (about 2 to 3 hours).

5. To unmold: Fill a large pan or sink with hot water. Hold the

mold in the water for 1 minute. Shake very gently. Place serving dish over mold and flip with one quick motion. Garnish with sweetened whipped cream. If desired, pipe whipped cream rosettes on soufflé top.

Raspberry Layer

¼ cup frozen orange juice concentrate, thawed
2 tablespoons unflavored gelatin
2 10-ounce boxes frozen raspberries, thawed and
   strained (reserve juice)
2 eggs, separated
¼ cup plus 2 tablespoons sugar
1 tablespoon bourbon

1. Pour orange juice over gelatin in a small bowl. Set aside to soften. In a heavy saucepan, combine gelatin and orange juice with raspberries, raspberry juice, egg yolks, and ¼ cup sugar. Cook over low heat, stirring constantly, until slightly thickened (about 4 minutes). Remove from heat and stir in bourbon. Set aside to cool.
2. Beat egg whites until soft peaks form. Gradually add remaining 2 tablespoons sugar, while continuing to beat, until stiff peaks form. Fold egg whites into raspberry mixture.

Cream Puffs
(Brandteigkrapferln)

MAKES 10 SERVINGS

Is there anyone who doesn't love cream puffs? With my basic cream puff dough and three delectable fillings—banana, chestnut, and coffee—cream puff lovers will have more to love.

Ideally, cream puffs should be filled as close to serving time as possible so they don't become soggy. If you must fill them several hours ahead of time, a powdered stabilizer called "Whip It" will stop the cream from weeping.

½ cup butter or margarine, cut into pieces
Dash of salt
½ cup milk
1 tablespoon sugar
1 cup flour
4 eggs
Desired Cream Puff Filling (recipes follow)
1 recipe Chocolate or Coffee Icing (see Index)

1. Preheat oven to 375°F. Butter and flour a baking sheet and set aside.

2. Heat butter, salt, and milk until butter melts. Add the sugar and flour and stir vigorously until mixture no longer sticks to pan. Remove from heat. Cool slightly.

3. Add eggs, one at a time, and beat well until blended. With a pastry bag or 2 spoons, form dough into round or oblong shapes on the prepared baking sheet. Place shapes about 2 inches apart. Bake in preheated 375°F. oven until golden and puffed (about 20 minutes). Remove from oven to cool on wire rack. Make a small slit in the sides of the puffs for steam to escape. When puffs cool, they can be filled right away or stored for several days in a cool spot.

4. Fill puffs by piping filling from a pastry bag through the small steam slit or by cutting off tops, spooning cream into puffs, then replacing tops. Spoon Chocolate or Coffee Icing over cream puffs and refrigerate until serving time.

Banana Whipped Cream Filling

2 ripe bananas
1 cup whipping cream
2 tablespoons confectioners' sugar
1 ⅓-ounce envelope "Whip It" (optional)
2 to 3 tablespoons crème de cacao or coffee liqueur

1. Mash bananas with a fork or in blender or food processor. Set aside.
2. Whip cream until soft peaks form. Gradually add sugar and optional stabilizer if desired. Whip until cream holds stiff peaks. Stir in bananas and liqueur. Taste and add more liqueur, if desired.

Chestnut Whipped Cream Filling

1 cup whipping cream
2 tablespoons confectioners' sugar
1 ⅓-ounce envelope "Whip It" (optional)
1 cup chestnut puree (*crème de marrons vanillée*)
2 to 3 tablespoons orange liqueur or coffee liqueur

Whip cream until soft peaks form. Gradually add sugar and optional stabilizer, if desired. Whip until cream holds peaks. Stir in chestnut puree and liqueur. Taste and add more liqueur, if desired.

Coffee Whipped Cream Filling

1 cup whipping cream
¼ cup confectioners' sugar
1 ⅓-ounce envelope "Whip It" (optional)
2 tablespoons instant coffee
2 to 3 tablespoons coffee liqueur or bourbon

Whip cream until soft peaks form. Gradually add sugar and optional stabilizer, if desired. Continue whipping until cream holds stiff peaks. Dissolve coffee in liqueur and stir into whipped cream. Taste and add more sugar and liqueur, if desired.

Steamed Chocolate Pudding with Whipped Cream
(Mohr im Hemd)

MAKES 12 SERVINGS

So many people tell me that this dessert—a soufflé-like steamed chocolate pudding—is the best dessert they've ever eaten. I always have the whipped cream waiting in the refrigerator to surround the hot pudding as soon as I turn it out of the mold. Of course, it must be served right away because the contrast of the hot, rich chocolate pudding with the cool whipped cream is fantastic.

1 cup semisweet chocolate morsels
¾ cup butter, at room temperature
1 cup sugar
7 eggs, separated
1 cup almonds, ground

Garnish
   2 cups whipping cream
   3 to 4 tablespoons confectioners' sugar

1. Generously butter and sugar a 6-cup steamed pudding mold. Shake out excess sugar. (If steamed pudding mold with lid is unavailable, use another 6-cup metal mold or even a heat-proof 6-cup bowl. Instead of a lid, cover mold with a double thickness of aluminum foil, sealing tightly.) Select a cooking pot large enough to hold the mold with about 2 inches of space on all sides. Fill the cooking pot with enough water to come halfway up the sides of the mold. Cover the pot and set over high heat. Set prepared mold aside.

2. Melt chocolate and set aside. Beat butter and sugar until fluffy. Add egg yolks, melted chocolate, and almonds. Mix to combine. Set aside. Beat egg whites until stiff. Fold into chocolate mixture. Pour mixture into prepared mold. Cover

with lid or double thickness of aluminum foil, pressing foil tightly around sides to seal.

3. When water boils, reduce heat and place the mold in the pot. Cover the pot with a tight-fitting lid. The water should remain at a gentle simmer for 1½ hours. Check several times during the steaming to make sure water is not boiling and to keep the water halfway up the sides of the mold. After 1½ hours, the heat can be turned off and the pudding can wait in the hot water bath for up to 60 minutes before serving.

4. Prepare whipped cream by beating cream until soft peaks form. Add confectioners' sugar and beat until cream holds stiff peaks.

5. To serve pudding: Remove mold from hot water bath and take off lid or foil. Place serving platter over mold. Grasp plate and mold in both hands and invert mold onto platter. Surround the pudding with whipped cream and serve right away. To serve, cut into 12 wedges.

Palatschinken
(*Crepes*)

MAKES 6 TO 8 SERVINGS

Palatschinken are the Austrian version of crepes. These thin pancakes are so delicious and versatile that many desserts can be made from one basic recipe. I have included three variations. In the first, the crepes are simply filled with jam and dusted with confectioners' sugar. In the second, the crepes are stuffed with a wonderful sour cream and raisin filling, then baked with a sour cream topping. The third recipe is a fancy Crepe Gâteau—crepes are layered with almonds, sugar, and raisins in a soufflé dish, then baked. The Gâteau is cut into wedges and served with a delicate vanilla sauce.

⅓ cup butter
2 cups flour
2 cups milk
2 egg yolks
¼ cup sugar
Dash salt
½ cup butter, for frying crepes

Garnish
    ½ cup raspberry or apricot jam
    Confectioners' sugar

1. Melt ⅓ cup butter. Set aside to cool.
2. Mix the melted butter, flour, milk, egg yolks, sugar, and salt with an electric mixer until smooth.
3. Place 1 tablespoon butter in a heavy 9- or 10-inch frying pan. Place over medium heat. When butter is very hot, pour enough batter to make a thin layer (about ⅛ inch) on bottom of pan. When crepe is brown on bottom, flip and cook other side until lightly browned. Remove from pan and put on plate. Cover to keep warm. Add another tablespoon butter to pan and continue as above until all crepes are fried. Cover after each addition to the cooked pile to keep crepes warm.
4. When all crepes are fried, fill each with 1 tablespoon jam. Roll or fold and dust with confectioners' sugar. Serve right away.

Palatschinken Baked with Sour Cream and Raisins
(Gebackene Palatschinken mit Rahm und Rosinen)

MAKES 6 TO 8 SERVINGS

Basic Palatschinken batter (see Index)
¼ cup butter, at room temperature
¼ cup confectioners' sugar
3 eggs, separated
½ cup sour cream
1 tablespoon flour
1 tablespoon dark raisins

Topping
   ½ cup sour cream
   2 egg yolks

1. Prepare basic Palatschinken batter. Fry crepes according to directions in Step 3. Do not cover crepes as each one is cooked, but let them cool.
2. Preheat oven to 350°F. Butter a 10″ × 6″ baking dish and set aside.
3. While crepes are cooling, prepare filling. Combine butter, confectioners' sugar, 3 egg yolks, ½ cup sour cream, flour, and raisins. Set aside. Beat egg whites until stiff and fold into filling. Spread filling evenly on crepes. Roll crepes and place in prepared baking dish. Make topping by mixing ½ cup sour cream with 2 egg yolks. Pour over crepes. At this point, the crepes can be covered and refrigerated for several hours before baking.
4. Bake crepes in preheated 350°F. oven until golden (about 25 minutes).

Crepe Gâteau with Almond Filling
(Palatschinken Auflauf)
MAKES 12 SERVINGS

      Basic Palatschinken batter (see Index)
      1 cup almonds, ground
      ½ cup sugar
      2 tablespoons dark raisins
      1 egg
      Peel of 1 orange, grated
      Vanilla Sauce (recipe follows)

1. Preheat oven to 350°F. Butter a 10-inch soufflé dish or other round baking dish. Set aside.

2. Prepare basic Palatschinken batter and fry crepes according to directions in Step 3. Do not cover crepes as each one is cooked, but let them cool.

3. Mix almonds, sugar, raisins, egg, and orange peel to combine. Place one crepe on bottom of soufflé dish and sprinkle with some filling. Add another crepe and more filling. Continue until all crepes and filling are used. At this point, crepes can be covered and refrigerated for several hours before baking.

4. Bake in preheated 350°F. oven until golden (about 35 to 40 minutes). To serve, cut into 12 wedges and serve with room temperature Vanilla Sauce.

Vanilla Sauce

      1 cup half-and-half
      1 cup sugar
      4 egg yolks
      1 teaspoon cornstarch
      1 2-inch length of vanilla bean
      ½ cup butter, at room temperature

1. Combine all ingredients but butter in a heavy saucepan and cook over low heat until sauce thickens. Stir sauce

constantly as it cooks. As soon as it thickens, remove from heat and continue stirring to cool slightly. Remove vanilla bean and set sauce aside.

2. With an electric mixer, beat butter until fluffy. Mix with sauce and set aside to cool to room temperature. Sauce can be made in advance and refrigerated. Bring to room temperature before serving.

Baked Noodle Dessert
(Nussnudeln)
MAKES 12 SERVINGS

This is my grandmother's original recipe. Served directly from the oven, it makes a wonderful family dessert on a blustery winter night. All you need to precede it is a hearty bowl of soup.

1 pound egg noodles, ½ inch wide
¼ cup butter
8 eggs, separated
¾ cup sugar
1½ cups nuts, ground
Peel of ½ orange, grated
Peel of ½ lemon, grated
2 teaspoons cinnamon
¼ cup dark raisins

1. Cook noodles according to package instructions. Drain thoroughly. Toss with butter and set aside to cool.
2. Preheat oven to 350° F. Butter an oven-proof, 2-quart glass or ceramic baking dish. Set aside.
3. Beat egg yolks with sugar, nuts, citrus peels, and cinnamon until just combined. Mix in raisins and set aside. Beat egg whites until stiff. Fold egg whites into reserved batter. Fold egg white mixture with reserved noodles. Taste and adjust seasoning if necessary. Pour into prepared baking dish and bake in preheated 350° F. oven until golden (about 20 to 30 minutes). The Nussnudeln can be left in the oven for up to 30 minutes (with heat turned off) before serving.

9

Buttercreams and Icings

These buttercream and icing recipes embellish so many of my dessert creations. They are quick to make, simple, and absolutely delicious. I always like to have icings and buttercreams on hand either in the refrigerator or in the freezer. With the buttercream and icing already made, I can whip up an elegant dessert like Chocolate Cake Roll in less than 40 minutes, start to finish.

Buttercreams that have been frozen or refrigerated should stand at room temperature for 30 minutes, then be whipped to refluff. Refrigerated icings should also be beaten smooth before using.

Buttercreams can be spread with a small metal spatula or spreader. Icings can be poured over cakes, then spread with a spatula to smooth. For small petits fours and cookies, it is sometimes easier to brush the icing on with a pastry brush. All of the recipes can be halved or doubled.

Coffee Buttercream
(Kaffeecreme)

4 egg yolks
3 tablespoons instant coffee dissolved in 2 tablespoons
     hot water or heated leftover coffee
1 cup butter, at room temperature
1½ cups confectioners' sugar
2 tablespoons bourbon or rum

1. In a heavy saucepan, cook egg yolks and coffee over low heat. Stir constantly until mixture thickens. Remove from heat right away. Set aside to cool.
2. Beat butter and sugar until light and fluffy. Mix cooled coffee mixture with sugar and butter. Add liquor and beat until creamy. Taste and add more sugar and liquor if desired.

Chestnut Buttercream
(Kastaniencreme)

4 egg yolks
1 17½-ounce can chestnut puree *(crème de marrons vanillée)*
½ cup semisweet chocolate morsels
1 cup butter, at room temperature
½ cup confectioners' sugar
2 to 3 tablespoons bourbon or rum

1. In a heavy saucepan, cook egg yolks, chestnut puree, and chocolate over low heat. Stir constantly until mixture thickens. Remove from heat right away. Set aside to cool.
2. Beat butter and sugar until light and fluffy. Beat in cooled chestnut mixture. Add liquor and beat until creamy. Taste and add more sugar and liquor if desired.

Chocolate Buttercream
(Schokoladencreme)

4 egg yolks
1 cup semisweet chocolate morsels
2 tablespoons instant coffee dissolved in 2 tablespoons
    water *or* 2 tablespoons leftover coffee
1 cup butter, at room temperature
1 cup confectioners' sugar
4 tablespoons bourbon or rum

1.   In a heavy saucepan, cook egg yolks, chocolate, and coffee over low heat. Stir constantly until mixture thickens. Remove from heat right away. Set aside to cool.
2.   Beat butter and sugar until light and fluffy. Mix cooled chocolate mixture with sugar and butter. Add liquor and beat until creamy. Taste and add more sugar and liquor if desired.

Chocolate Icing
(Schokoladenguss)

½ cup butter
1 cup semisweet chocolate morsels

1.   Melt butter in a small heavy saucepan. Add chocolate to butter. Remove from heat and stir until smooth. Let cool until icing is of spreading consistency.
2.   To melt refrigerated icing: Cook over very low heat, stirring constantly, just until chocolate melts. Remove from heat and let cool until icing is of spreading consistency.

Lemon or Orange Icing
(Zitronen oder Orangen Guss)

2 cups confectioners' sugar
1½ tablespoons egg white (about ½ an egg white)
⅓ cup orange or lemon juice concentrate, thawed
Peel of ½ orange or 1 lemon, grated

Beat all ingredients for 5 minutes. Scrape down sides of bowl occasionally so icing is smooth.

Coffee Icing
(Kaffeeguss)

2 cups confectioners' sugar
1½ tablespoons egg white (about ½ an egg white)
2 tablespoons instant coffee dissolved in 2 tablespoons
    hot water *or* 2 tablespoons leftover coffee

Beat all ingredients at high speed for 5 minutes. Scrape down sides of bowl occasionally so icing is smooth.

10

Plan a "Baking Day" for a Special Party

It's rather easy to make one impressive dessert for a sit-down dinner, but if you have a large buffet and really want to do something special for dessert, set aside one day for a "Baking Day." By following my plan, you can prepare enough beautiful petits fours or bite-size sweets for fifty guests. When placed in tiny paper cups and presented on trays, the petits fours look divine and I guarantee they will taste that way too.

The "Baking Day" can take place up to a week before the party. The pastries can be refrigerated, well-wrapped in aluminum foil or in a tin. Make a list of all ingredients and shop several days before or early on the morning of the "Baking Day." Check the list several times. It's annoying and time-consuming to interrupt your baking to run to the store.

The following list is a selection that has worked well for me, but please feel free to develop a different plan of your own.

1. Bake Eggwhite Chocolate Cake (page 32)

2. With leftover egg yolks, make two recipes of buttercream. Choose Chocolate, Coffee, or Chestnut Buttercreams (pages 102–103) or make one recipe each of two different kinds for variety.

3. Make a Lemon Cake Roll (page 16) and a Walnut Cake Roll (page 18).

4. Mix Ischler Cookie dough (page 70) and refrigerate.

5. Make a triple recipe of Chocolate Icing (page 103), one recipe Coffee Icing (page 104), and one recipe desired icing (for Chocolate Petits Fours); set icings aside to cool.

6. Roll Ischler dough; cut, bake, and cool cookies.

7. Make Chocolate Petits Fours (page 64).

8. Cut the Lemon and Walnut Cake Rolls to make four rolls. Spread with buttercream. Roll jelly-roll fashion and cover two rolls with Coffee Icing and two with Chocolate Icing.

9. Cover Eggwhite Chocolate Cake with Chocolate Icing. Use remaining Chocolate Icing to decorate Ischler Cookies.

10. Assemble Chocolate Petits Fours and frost with desired icing.

11. Wrap pastries well and refrigerate. (Baking can also be done weeks in advance and pastries wrapped and frozen).

12. On the day of the party (up to two hours in advance), cut the Lemon and Walnut Cake Rolls into slices. Place each slice in a small paper cup. Cut the Eggwhite Chocolate Cake into slices and cut each slice in half. Arrange on trays in a pretty design along with Ischler cookies and Chocolate Petits Fours. Cover with plastic wrap. Refrigerate until serving time.

Index